I0156456

# THE FOG IS GONE

### *An Ex-Pastors' Experience of Seeing Past Christianity to Enlightenment*

By

## Temel Karango

Forward by Jah Ranu Menab

# The Fog Is Gone
## An Ex-Pastors' Experience of Seeing Past Christianity to Enlightenment

by Temel Karango

### Published by

### Stellar Sol Publishing

### PO BOX 752972 Las Vegas, NV 89136

www.temelkarango.com

No part of this book may be reproduced in any form or by any electronic or mechanical means, including information storage and retrieval systems, without permission from the publisher, except as permitted by U.S. copyright law.

For permissions contact:
Attention "Permissions coordinator" at: www.temelkarango.com

Copyright © 2018 by Temel Karango
All rights reserved.

ISBN-13:978-0692081792 (Paperbook)
ISBN-10:0692081798

Cover Design By: Christina Paraskevopoulou
Interior Design By: Shehu, A

The Fog Is Gone
An Ex-Pastors' Experience of Seeing Passed Christianity to Enlightenment
Karango, Temel
Printed and Bound in USA Stellar Sol Publishing 2018

Stellar Sol
PUBLISHING

*This book is dedicated to the memory of my parents, Carlyn and Nate McCrary I, who taught me how to be real and to live out my dreams. You guide me still on my life's voyage, and you will be forever celebrated, adored, and loved as my direct creators and ancestors.*

# Forward

Temel Karango sprang into my life in 1989 on the campus of Moody Bible Institute (MBI) in Chicago, Illinois, where we studied for our bachelor's degrees. He exhibited all the tell-tale signs of a new convert to the Christian faith: unquenchable zeal, dogged determination, undefeatable idealism. He also brought a refreshing attitude toward matriculation into the overwhelmingly white student body: unmitigated blackness!

By the time TK arrived, I had founded the Afro Awareness Fellowship, a support group exclusively for black students. TK soon became my vice president and successor. We both used different names back then. We graced the campus in the wake of MBI's 100th anniversary. "Moody," as the world-renowned college was known, was the first and greatest bastion of evangelicalism and Protestant Christian fundamentalism in America. "The sun never set on a Moody student," the saying went, extolling the vast reach of the institution through its training of missionaries and its mass media outreach.

"Oh, he's not a Christian, he's Catholic," a student or staff member would describe some public figure. This is just one example of how fringe this group was. Many even believed the Pope was the Anti-Christ. The school's ultra-conservative position permeated not only its theological teachings, it reached into every aspect of campus life. Conservatism in America means racism.

Institutional racism at MBI had no better home than its teachings on church history. Students would leave class thinking all the characters in the Bible were white, from Adam to Moses to Jesus to John, except for a few insignificant souls here and there. All the church "fathers" were white, they taught—implicitly and explicitly. I will never forget asking one of my professors, who had written a textbook on church history, why we never hear about blacks' contribution to the development of the church. "Hmm. I'll get back to you on that," he assured. A few weeks later he reported to me, "I couldn't find any."

Dumbfounded by his ignorance, I just walked away shaking my head. I already knew that most of the Bible characters were explicitly black—even the Israelites. I already knew that Nubia was the first nation to adopt Christianity as its national religion—even before Roman Emperor Constantine convened the Nicaean Counsel. I already knew that most of the prominent bishops of the early church were blacks of Ethiopia and Egypt—even Augustine and Turtulian. I already knew that 5 of the early popes were black. I already knew that African scribes wrote most of the extant Greek and Latin Bible manuscripts—even the most complete New Testament manuscript, Codex Alexandrinus, was written in black Egypt, the Egypt before the Arab Muslim conquest that turned North Africa white many centuries later.

But why did our professors not know? Or did they? These facts were not hard for TK and me to find. It also was not hard for us to discover that Moody was only typical of American and white Christianity worldwide as far as race relations were concerned.

Through "The Fellowship," as we often referred to our student organization, our black schoolmates became intimately acquainted with many of the most prominent black fundamentalist leaders in the country. They were the vanguards our people of faith in a most segregated institution of American society—church. They had created black councils, associations, parachurch organizations and other enterprises to serve the needs of our people when "mainstream" (code for "white") Christian institutions neglected us.

Not least among these leaders was evangelist Rev. Tom Skinner. Known globally as "The Black Billy Graham" because of his notoriety in the 1960s and '70s, Skinner enjoyed spending quality time with Fellowship members. When he came to Chicago, the guys would book a hotel room where he stayed and camped out all night eating, talking, and sharing our hearts and hopes with him. Skinner had been the one black evangelical that Moody and other white mass media producers allowed to occupy time and space in their radio, TV and print media. There was only room, it seemed, for one black man at a time. His keynote address at Urbana '70, virtually a Christian version of Woodstock, entitled "The US Racial Crisis and World Evangelism" must have fallen on deaf ears, because InterVarsity Christian Fellowship, the company that organizes Urbana events, posted in its pre-Urbana '18 promotional website, "Over four decades later, Skinner's words still ring with prophetic clarity today." "Prophetic," huh? That means they still don't get it. Although Urbana '90 was located in nearby Urbana, Illinois, only one or two of our Fellowship members attended. Most others were not even interested in going.

We met Rev. Dr. Anthony "Tony" Evans, too, then the heir-apparent to Skinner's singular black voice in American Christian media. We were not nearly as impressed. Dr. Evans turned us off when he came to campus with his gung-ho charge that helped raise hundreds of millions of US dollars to bolster mission projects into East Germany following the fall of the Berlin Wall while we were walking across the street every week into Cabrini Green. This is one of Chicago's most famous and most deplorable housing projects, full of our people who needed to see meaningful economic resources from Christian ministry to feel its relevance. Cabrini did not get a dime from Evans' "urban" ministry.

Our group provided spiritual, intellectual, social and psychological support to our young brothers and sisters on campus to avert or rescue them from identity crises that could—and often did—ensue from the white supremacist context that beset us. Much of this support poured in from local leaders of national evangelical organizations which had been established in response to the lock-out of black leadership and cultural expression from major white organizations. The relationships we cultivated with our local sages was deep and close.

Eminent black theologian, author, pastor, intellect Dr. William H. "Bill" Bentley was one of these giants. He was one of the founders of one of the largest organizations of its kind. Disciples throughout the nation affectionately named him "Father of the National Black Evangelical Association." Dr. Bentley and his wife Dr. Ruth Bentley worked feverishly rallying college students around the socio-economic relevance to black people of the Gospel of Jesus Christ. I was awe-struck every time they invited me to their home. There, I found soulful meals, historical artifacts, thought-provoking and strategic conversation, and, as legend had it, the most vast library of black theology and sociology in the nation. Getting to know the Bentley's beautiful twin daughters better added a much-appreciated social element to our relationship, as well.

The Bentleys and others formed The National Black Evangelical Association (NBEA) in the 1963 due to the systemic ethnic negligence of its majority-white counterpart, National Evangelical Association (NEA). The Fellowship participated fervently in NBEA conferences. One of our shining moments was standing on the NEA-NBEA Joint Commission on Race Relations, which held congress in Chicago, and signing our names as co-contributors to the official position paper that resulted from that historic event.

In 1993, Fellowship members attended the funeral of Dr. Bill *en masse*. The church home of Rev. Walter Arthur McCray hosted the services. McCray was one of the chief organizers of the Christian African American Booksellers Association, formed due to the ethnic negligence of its majority-white counterpart, the Christian Booksellers Association, the largest

Christian trade organization in the bookselling industry. McCray was the author of the Black Presence in the Bible series, a scholarly work revealing the Black African identities of nearly all significant individuals and peoples of the Old and New Testaments. He was a friend of the Fellowship and opened his home to us and visited our campus often. His works and thoughts indelibly shaped TK's and my perspective on biblical and church history and constantly begged the question, "Why the cover-up?" Why are nearly all white and even so many black Christians resolved to proclaiming, "It doesn't matter what color they were! All that matters is Jesus saves!"?

Rev. Russell Knight spent many hours on campus guiding and mentoring our students. He also led us into grimy neighborhoods weekly to minister to our people. A Moody graduate himself, Knight established CURE, one of the largest Christian youth ministries in the Midwest. He and his Caucasian wife Beth (also a Moody grad) swung their doors wide open for our college crowd and scores of youth from the economically impoverished black and Latino neighborhood on the Southside of Chicago, where they lived and sent their children to public schools. During weekends and school breaks, the Knight home was our home. There, we saw the true power of urban ministry.

At the time of this writing, Knight, McCray and Dr. Ruth Bentley served on the NBEA board of directors.

On the West Side, Rev. Clarence Hilliard led a pastors' alliance. A vibrant NBEA member, Hilliard was committed to enriching black Moody students and exposing us to and preparing us for ministry on his side of town. His famous 1976 essay, *Down with the Honky Christ; Up with the Funky Jesus* published in Christianity Today, the internationally-circulated magazine that Billy Graham "built" (according to one of its former presidents), had thrust him onto the front lines of warfare for theological race reconciliation. To express his endearment to the Fellowship, Hilliard and his wife Annie were among the few non-family members who attended my graduation, and they presented me with a memorable gift.

Other celebrated local evangelical leaders embraced us. One was Rev. Dr. Jeremiah Wright. The world knows him most as President Barak Obama's former pastor. Wright's Trinity United Church of Christ is where the aspiring attorney honed some of his grassroots organizing and social action skills that prepared him for national leadership. It was Wright's 1988 alter call through which Obama came into the Faith. That was my freshman year at Moody.

Shortly after that, Fellowship members and I became more acquainted with Dr. Wright. Some of us joined Trinity. I will never forget how he drove me back to campus one day in his slick black Porsche with all-black leather interior. That kind of spontaneous one-on-one interaction with people of great influence was common for TK and other Fellowship students.

Undoubtedly the most famous local figure to connect with the Fellowship was Donald Campbell. Readers may commonly know him by his show business moniker, "Bishop Don Magic Juan." Shock and awe filled the auditorium as Bishop preached chapel to the entire student body in a once-in-a-lifetime experience. One of my evangelism professors, Dr. Rasher, had led the legendary pimp and hip-hop icon to Christ and helped him plant a short-lived, yet undeniable congregation on Chicago's west side. That is how and when Magic appropriated the title of "Bishop." The Bishop was sure to spend a little time with Fellowship members before leaving campus. Afterward, as I will always remember, a few of us walked him from deep within the campus to the street, where one of his bodyguards had been carefully standing watch over his money-green Cadillac Coupe DeVille.

In the mid-1990s, Corby Bush, one of the black staff workers at Moody, recruited TK and me to plant a church in his house on the West Side. TK gave the church its name—Light of Liberty, after his church home in Ohio. Pastor Bush incorporated the church under the diocese of the Church of God in Christ (COGIC) and installed TK and me as elders. TK performed many ministerial and evangelism duties and I preached and co-hosted the radio ministry. We helped Pas. Bush expand the church until it acquired a magnificent edifice in opulent Oak Park, Illinois, just outside Chicago city lines. We were laboring together there when COGIC Presiding Bishop Louis Henry Ford, of whom Bush was a beloved protégé, returned to the Lord. The church still grows today and Bush is actually a *bona fide* bishop in that, the largest African American denomination, having planted and now presiding over congregations in two states.

Pas. Bush was always politically involved, and probably had the most influence on Fellowship family toward taking political action. One thing that perplexed me was how conservative Christians could claim that one issue alone—abortion, specifically—could decide all votes for all candidates in all elections. At that time, it seemed that Republicans played the "right-to-life" card to harvest the Christian bloc. Somehow, I wondered if that party practice was only a propaganda device. I wondered if, behind that anti-abortion issue, well-to-do white evangelicals found comfort in the social and economic positions for which the Good Ol' Party stood.

Not far into my post-graduate life, the primary race for candidates for governor of Illinois offered all pro-choice Republicans and one pro-life Democrat. Instead of cutting party ties to rally around the single pro-lifer, evangelicals only met the media with silence on the issue. It was the same silence blacks heard throughout our history in America from conservative Christians. This race finally exposed to me the farce of political action in the name of God white evangelical leaders propagate. They false flag their white supremacy with more palatable issues.

Hypocrisy in political and social action, in judicial and economic justice, and even in teaching historical facts, drove me to find answers behind the fictions about God upon which my Christian upbringing seemed to be built.

My mind was in a fog.

It was my study of history that fetched the answers I sought. During my college years and beyond, my incessant study of history disclosed what any reasonable, objective person can only conclude to be deliberately-hidden facts that led Christianity to where it is today.

From the time of Emperor Constantine I, who created the Christian religion and Bible as we know it today, elite whites have used the Faith to subject massive populations to their rule in their own territories an throughout the world, and to a amass unspeakable fortunes through plunder, social engineering and political machinations.

In the USA, black labor created white wealth. The labor was free at first, then Republicans changed that; blacks flocked to them. Democrats created the Ku Klux Klan anti-black terrorist organization and instituted Jim Crow to *conserve* as much of the *status quo* as possible. Conservative Christians filled their ranks—especially in the South, and especially among the Southern Baptists, then largest Protestant denomination in the country. The church underscored the conservative rhetoric of the party.

After Democratic President Franklin Delano Roosevelt's New Deal began to lure our people into his party with economic incentives in the 1930s, it was the infusion, proliferation and influence of former Nazi party white supremacist scientist within the leadership of the Republican party that pushed nearly two thirds of our voters into the Democratic party by 1960. Whatever remnant of our people remained in the Republican party almost completely migrated by 1964, when

Sen. Barry Goldwater (A.K.A. "Mr. Conservative") took the Republican presidential nomination with his Klan-like rhetoric. That remnant helped defeat Goldwater, yet Republicans Richard Nixon and Ronald Reagan used Goldwater's "Southern Strategy" to win blocs of conservative Christian votes and, accordingly, to win their presidencies.

As I studied beyond this nation, I traced the spread of Christianity and saw similar and even more devilish atrocities and hypocrisy almost everywhere Christianity had spread. I left the Faith and became a Muslim. History also led to my discovery of the African origin of Arabic religion and writing. It, too, uncovered the brazen hypocrisy of Arab Muslims' conquest, genocide and enslavement throughout North Africa, where they continue their slave trade unrestrained to this very day, and their centuries of ethnic cleansing of their own race and others. It, too, had only been used by its elite leadership as a weapon of geopolitical mass destruction and wealth aggregation.

Finally, my research into the formation of the *original* nation of Israel cleared the fog of my religious frustration. I learned through the texts of today's so-called "Jewish" and Muslim scholars that the biblical Israelite nation was a kingdom of Northeast African refugees who had been exiled from Egypt for following a heretic king and his high priest who instituted a foreign religious philosophy introduced by his foreign wife. The exiles found refuge among Canaanites and adopted much of their language and fabricated their "history" (what we call the Books of Moses in the Old Testament) by codifying the history of the kings of Egypt and substituting Canaanite names for those of prominent Egyptian figures.

The one thing that the three major world religious traditions have in common is their origin in and dependence upon Black Africa.

Studying the ancient Nile Valley spiritual system, its influence on all major and most other religions, and the history of the migrations and marine travel of Black Africans throughout the Dark Continent and around the world for hundreds of thousands of years before any other race of people even existed supplied me with only one logical conclusion: The ancient Black African spiritual system is the original and longest-lasting source of light, civilization, science, high culture, peace and prosperity on the planet; therefore, it is the one I need to learn, apply and master.

TK, though taking a different route after leaving COGIC, has come to the same conclusion. In this, his initial volume and certainly the first-fruit of many, he seeks to provide a guide for others through and out of the fog.

Jah Ranu Menab

Chicago, February 23, 2018

# Preface

I was over half way finished with another book that I was writing, called Hank, Bill, and Sam. This book was addressing, what I believe, to be the only relevant discussion surrounding race in America, reparations. I went to Chicago to do a radio and television interview, and as opposed to having interview questions surrounding the book I was prepared to discuss, all the questions addressed to me were concerning what caused me to leave the ministry. This was surprising as it had been over 10 years that I had left the pastorate.

During these interviews, I hosted a town hall meeting called "The Meeting of The Minds." On this diverse panel was myself, a Christian Pastor James Ford, my Muslim Brother Michal Muhammed, and my Conscience Sister Kimistry Awake. In our attempt to look at diverse aspects of approaching our issues in the Black culture, the overall concern from the audience was the influence of religion on Black people. People were intrigued at my transformation from a Christian pastor to now an Awakened leader for Black people.

On my way back home to Las Vegas from Chicago, I was reflecting on how everywhere I went, the topic of interest was always surrounding me being a formal pastor. Organically, I thought about the timing of my book Hank, Bill, and Sam. It seemed natural and I realized that it would only make sense to write about what everyone was craving to know about me first. After coming to this resolve, I postponed Hank, Bill, and Sam, and the idea for this book The Fog Is Gone immediately came into mind.

To write this book required a lot of memory research. Which because of my past experiences having some painful episodes, this was an emotional exploit. This book is a biographical sketch of my life detailing specifically my experiences with Christianity. With that being said, the very reason most of us from the hood come to Christianity and specifically those who haven't grew up in church, is because we have grown up in some extreme pains in need of relief. Christianity and the church is sometimes the only positive outlet that we have.

The main reasons for writing this book are threefold. The chief reason is to create a serious dialogue on Western religion's (Christianity in particular) grip on the Black culture, and addressing it is as the leading obstruction to us becoming a high culture. Secondly, to awaken the minds of those who feel bound to religion and see it impossible to live without it. Lastly, but as equally important, is that this book is a sort of redemption for the unfair criticism and evil expressed towards me after renouncing my religious beliefs and ministry.

This book is highly controversial and is the first of its kind. However contentious this book may prove to be, it is my sacrifice and honour to present my personal experience as a formal Christian and pastor. I think you will find this read to be credibly insightful from someone who had a deep and devout commitment to Christianity and had a provocative departure from the entire belief system.

# Table of Contents

# THE FOG IS GONE

*An Ex-Pastors' Experience of Seeing
Past Christianity to Enlightenment*

# CHAPTER ONE

## *What in the Fog*

"Nicky, you're not a baby anymore; you're walking and talking now so I need you to be on your best behavior. Your dad and I are only going to be gone for a couple of days and you and your sister are going to stay at your aunt Maries." I thundered in outburst "Aw ma, no! I don't wanna go over to Aunt Marie's house!" I pronounced my aunt's name as "Aint Marie," with my face running a faucet of tears, whining in an extreme temper tantrum.

Carlyn snapped back at me, "Shut your little ass up, I don't want to hear nothing else about it, you're going over your

1

aunt's house for a few days and that's that, damn it!" Defiantly sniffling, I turned to my older sister with a whimpering whisper and short breath and said "Debbie, I don't wanna go!" As a big sister, older by over 4 years would irritatingly say to her brat of a much younger brother, "Quit crying and stop being a punk!"

In the mid to late 70's, not only were there no personal computers, laptops, or cell phones, there were also no strict laws on car seats for young children or seat belt infractions. This was a time cars had eight track tapes and you literally had to roll the windows up and down. By the way, Michael Jackson was on his way to running the music world at this time.

In the back seat of the car that my dad had bought my mom, I would stand and look out the window at everything new and familiar. The car was a two door, maroon leather interior; silver exterior 70's something Buick Regal. I was just becoming angrier as we were approaching some of the people's houses and buildings I knew from my aunt's and uncle's block. At last, the dreaded pulling up to that building where my aunt Marie and Uncle Motley lived gave me a feeling of awfulness.

This building I later learned was owned by my dad was off Central Avenue on the east side of Cleveland, Ohio. In the 70's to 80's, and later 90's, clearly exemplified the true transition nationwide from the neighborhood to the hood.

The building was built in the early 1900's and was a few stories high with a shotgun style duplex structure. For a three to four year old who was about to separate from his parents, it became the haunted house where I felt my parents would leave me and my sister forever and ever.

I gave my last plea and protest. "Mommy, can we just stay at my Aunt Debbie's house?" My aunt Debbie was my mom's much younger sister. Aunt Debbie, who lived in a more upscale neighborhood for that time near East Cleveland, always made sure we were having fun. I spent more time and connected more with my aunt Debbie because she was young and my cousin Caprice was just a few months older than me.

We were always going to the theatre, drive-in, the mall, and short trips. See, my aunt Debbie, who my sister was named after, was always making us cookies, cakes and other unnameable delicacies. I was just thrilled to be able to think of and propose such a great alternative for my mom rather than going into my aunt's and uncle's house.

Strongly believing that I was suggesting to Carlyn a new clever and creative idea; "mom can we; can we just stay at Aunt Debbie's house?" Carlyn, slow but articulately clear and sharp, "No you can't! Your aunt has plans this weekend. But what you're going to do is, take your little ass in your aunt's and uncle's house, and you better not tear shit up, or I'm going to tear your little ass up when I get back. Do you understand me?" Whiffling at one hundred breathes per second I stutteringly responded, "Ye ye yes, mama mam."

Aunt Marie and Uncle Motley were lovingly inviting as we came into their home. After settling in good, Debbie who never held her tongue about nothing, looked at me and said in a hush lipless motion as our noses both experienced the whiff of oddness, "it smells like old people." For me at that age, it was truly awful.

I felt abandoned and hopeless, completely spectrum opposite from Aunt Marie's exuberance to have young life around. Uncle Motley had more of what you would call a short tolerance for "young folk." He would always be didactic in his interactions with us. It was always a lesson in the story being told. He would always explain how "God is in everything we do, and don't nothing happen without God knowing or controlling it."

That night, trying to fall asleep without my mom and dad around was horrific. The bedroom that Debbie and I slept in was off of the dining room. My aunt and uncle' bedroom was in the front of the house off the living room. Going to sleep and later waking up in an unfamiliar room feeling nothing like home felt like a nightmare.

The wooden head and foot board of the huge king size bed was a heavy and dark carefully crafted oak. It took a fist full of covers just to get up on the bed because the height was equal to three stacked mattresses. There were at least four to five layers of covers on the bed. There was the sheet, the undercover, the cover, the spread, the quilt, and some extra covers at the foot of the bed. Everything in the room was neatly in its place, with furnishings and trinkets time capsuling the early to mid-1900s.

Waking up for the first time in my aunt's and uncle's house was a new awkwardness. My eyes changing from blurring to perception, with the inner conflict of pleasure as I smelled the most delicious aroma coming from the kitchen. There was no trace of Debbie as she had already left out of the room.

Sliding cautiously out and down what felt like a five foot bed, I ran anxiously looking for Debbie who was helping Aunt Marie prepare breakfast. I sat down quietly at the kitchen table observant as my aunt was trying to engage me, "good morning baby, did you sleep good?" I, nodding my head indicating yes, had no intention of opening my mouth until I ate my steaming grits with freshly melted butter, half cut beef sausages, cheese eggs, with butter fried wheat toast topped with strawberry spread.

I was so anxious to eat but realized that we could not eat until we were given the green light. At the head of the table, Uncle Motley asked "do y'all know how to say grace?" Looking shamelessly to my Aunt Marie as we were clueless to the practice, he made me and Debbie bow our heads, close our eyes, and say "thank you" to someone I couldn't see before we could eat. He was passionate and was really saying "thank you" with great feeling. I was sure that when I snuck and opened my eyes, I would catch whoever he was talking to standing somewhere in the room.

Shortly after a few bites in, Aunt Marie began to explain to us that after breakfast, we needed to get dressed and be ready to go to church. "Church?" I looked at Debbie with confusion because I didn't know where they said we were going when referring to "church." I shrugged my shoulders and was just glad to be going anywhere away from their house.

I was puzzled on how I was going to have fun wearing the suit my aunt mysteriously knew that my mom had packed in my bag. I never needed to wear a suit before. On top of that, because we were just within walking distance from the church, having on a suit with dress shoes made this the longest and most uncomfortable hike ever.

Walking through the door of the store front church, I immediately knew this was not going to be a place for kids. Inside it was poorly lit, cold and stale. There was a partitioned walk way up the middle aisle between several rows of chairs. Looking straight ahead was a podium and mic with three bigger chairs in the back. These chairs were all elevated up a few feet from the other lined and rowed chairs. It appeared very organized and ordered, with no swings, slides, toys, cake, candy, or anything children our age would be remotely interested in.

Debbie and I kept eye checking each other with bewilderment as we had never met any of these new people who seemed to already know my Aunt and Uncle. At first it seemed that they didn't know my uncle's name because they kept calling him reverend. "Reverend" I thought? Who are they talking about? Debbie eventually tried to help me understand, in a big sister matter of fact way, she said "he a preacher, they call him preacher." I responded back "what's a preacher?" Debbie turned away in frustration and said "just forget it!"

There were no other children who came to church. I looked at Debbie extremely upset because I knew that we were doomed to some shenanigans. It was a very small membership with mostly elderly people. As my young body sat in my seat I observed members singing, moaning and sporadic outburst of cries out "Jesus!" In unison, there were men closing their eyes in uncontrollable surges of words, while women were shaking, gyrating, fainting, and hollering. For a child it was shocking and basically frightening.

My uncle sat in middle seat of the bigger elevated chairs directly behind the podium. He occasionally rose up with everyone joining in song and would sit back down. Eventually, he got up and asked for silence and had everyone close their eyes again.

With everyone's head bowed and eyes closed, having nothing else fun to do, I competed with myself that this time I would surely catch who my uncle was talking to now. I failed to catch him earlier when my uncle was talking to him before breakfast. This time though, with all these other people closing their eyes, I would just keep my eyes open and certainly catch him right when they said again, "he's in this place."

Needless to say, I didn't catch who he or they were talking to this time either. Talking to someone invisible, putting on an uncomfortable suit, sitting still for hours while having this large book with no pictures, was torture to me. Never having been to church one time with Nate Baby and Carlyn, I didn't know what in the fog a prayer, a preacher, a reverend, or a church even was.

# CHAPTER TWO

## *Before the Fog*

Recalling the earlier years of my life seem so cliché as these were some of the most pleasantly memorable years with my parents. Nate and Carlyn were not religious in the least, they were just real and they were mine. They owned a three bedroom two story house on Cleveland, Ohio's eastside.

When we were young, my parents took us all around the country. We had close family in Chicago, Detroit, Saint Louis, New York, Los Angeles, and Atlanta, which I have at some point lived in mostly all of these above named cities. We would go on vacations from Disney World all

9

the way to Canada, and it seemed like we would build the most picturesque family life forever.

My dad grew up in Taylor County south of Atlanta. When I was young, I went and visited where my dad grew up in Butler, Georgia and I couldn't believe I had hundreds of cousins in school who were still picking cotton for half a day. I was born when my dad was in his mid-forties, so he had already lived and seen so much life. This element of southern Blacks still trapped in Jim Crow practices disturbed me in my soul even as pre-teen.

After seeing where he grew up, and where we were growing up, I later understood why he kept so many guns all over the house as if we were waiting for the white sheets to walk in. Nonetheless, he was always the least rattled, with the least words, the least threatening, yet the most prepared. He always kept money and he took care of his family and his business.

My father's father (Grandfather) was a medicine man and went and healed all over the south. He helped cure people in the Carolinas, Georgia, Alabama, and Mississippi. From my Uncle Lou and Aunt Theo in Chicago, to my Aunt Pauline and Uncle TJ in Cleveland, they were still mainly southern in their ways and were naturally down to earth people. On my father's side of the family, you could be you. Everyone would cheer you on so that you could be the best that you could possibly be, with no condemnation if you fail short of expectations.

Carlyn's side of the family on the other hand was from the east coast. The Williams were very formal, strict, and disciplined. There was held exact family expectations with real consequences for non-achievement, especially for the boys. As far as the girls were concerned, the verdict from Carlyn was that she and my aunt Debbie received worse discipline with stricter moral adherences than her brothers.

My mom, her much younger sister, and her two older brothers were born to my grandparents Carl and Marie Williams. My mom would say to me in an indignantly reminiscent tone, "your grandmother and grandfather would kill me and your aunt Debbie, but they would kill for your uncles Bobby and Stan."

She had explained several times that there was a difference in treatment and expectations for the boys over girls in her family element. Though she became a registered nurse, she felt that she was still not accomplished to my grandparent's standards. The dynamic of her upbringing propelled her to be rebellious in her approach towards life. Carlyn would not be controlled again by anyone.

My mom being much younger than my dad, reared on the east coast and having very different experiences than my dad, she was a fire storm for my emotionally guarded and calm natured father. If we had a big party at our house, my mom would get sauced. After or sometimes before everyone left, Al Green would be playing loudly, Carlyn would start talking more shit than a little bit! Nate Baby would try to calm my mom as he was called all kind of M F's, and heard repeated mantras of "I don't give a Fs!"

Looking back, I now know my mom loved my dad but had been hurt by what she knew about him greatly different than what I could imagine. Nate Baby's side of the family now tells me all the time how my dad would always keep a fine car and a fine woman. I'm sure that's why some of the hurled MF's Nate Baby received by Carlyn happened. As I was seeing the rawest of pain and anger displayed without filter, surely it helped shape my temperament towards life growing up.

Unlike my cousins born to my uncles on my mom side, who grew up suburban and rigid and very similar to how my mom, aunt, and uncles grew up. Debbie and I grew up in the "hood." More pointedly, we grew up with a mom who resented and rebelled against how she was raised. My first communal memories, are those growing up in a neighborhood with Black owned corner stores and small retail businesses. Then, everybody knew everybody and there was a real sense of community.

Black music captured the era with songs from Marvin Gaye, Frankie Beverly, and the Ojays. The gangsters were refined and relatively respectful toward children and the elderly. Hiphop was in its beginning stages. Affiliations with organizations, gangs, or sets were primarily for protection of certain areas of interests or turfs. Violence was mostly reserved for gross violations. With all the seeming dangers of growing up in our all black neighbourhood, it quickly changed into a past paradise.

The shift was swift and traumatic. Without context or warning, we went from proud Black community to New Jack City. The eighties cultural warfare began, and the government flooded our streets with drugs and g u n s . There was the unbelievably sudden change from neighbourhood to the hood.

I was very young when I saw crack hit the block. Too young to evade it's devastating effects. From people who I knew and loved since a small kid becoming zombies in the night, to close family members succumbing to its addictions on both-sides, selling and abusing. There was family throughout the Midwest getting addicted, destroying their families, getting locked up, or killed behind its affects.

We had long suffered through seeing some of our own loved ones battling cocaine, heroin, and alcohol and thought nothing could be worse. Crack cocaine was worse. My house, like so many other Black families in my neighborhood, had turned from an aspiring family home to a trap house. I literally saw crack smack the neighbor right out of the hood!

By age thirteen, I felt that I had seen it all, felt it all, and done it all. My life experiences had accelerated way beyond my age. I didn't care about fighting anybody, wins or loses. Actually, I never thought that I would live to see sixteen years old. I kept my dad's Thirty-Eight for the real drama. I knew how to make money on the streets. I could drive and steal cars. I knew what grams and ounces were. I never smoked cocaine and only drank heavy occasionally, but I grew up smoking plenty of marijuana.

Because of the major turn in my family's dynamic, I lived by no one's rules. My girlfriends could stay in my bedroom at my house overnight. Smoking, drinking, or chilling in the house was not off limits. All structure was gone.

So much so, school felt so irrelevant in this type of environment. I would only go to school for a couple of hours, if that, and I was out the door again. So many people around me were going through some of the worst circumstances ever. There were so many young people dying, and so many family members in pain and crying. Just surviving became something congratulatory.

One day when cutting school with my cousin and a couple of my boys sitting at my kitchen table, my boy Ahmad, who I knew since we were babies came in the kitchen with tears in his eyes. We called Ahmad "Mod" growing up. "What's wrong Mod?" I asked. He looked at me stunned and hurt and said, "He dead man, they killed him!" "Killed who" I yelled? Ahmad said, "Looney! Looney just got killed!" "They shot him twice in the head and robbed him." Ahmad soon after explained all the details before we left my house to follow up on what happened. I had just seen Looney and was telling him to get off of 131st and Corlett selling work.

Every winter to every summer was an eternity and we seemed that we were all separating more and more by life's choices and circumstances. We had witnessed and knew plenty of the murderers and the murdered. Mod represented the 6 point star and Looney was a Vice Lord, rivals by affiliation. These differences didn't stop the pain and love Mod felt for Looney when he got murdered.

Looney was like a brother to me and at one time we did everything together. From the streets to Hiphop we mobbed together. We would knock out or take somebody out together. Through Hiphop we would demolish any so called challenging emcees. Mod would produce, Bat Mite and Will would DJ, while Looney and I were some of the coldest rappers in Hiphop period. All together we were the Legion of Doom.

Amid daily gang violence, antagonistic police patrolling, family members and close friends turned to fiends, schools ran like the jail house, no more Black businesses, and blatantly no more community bright future. Nihilism became normal for me and many young Black men as the meaning of life and hope of better days wasn't even a thought. That type of thinking did nothing but cause mental suffering. We had to survive and from that, learn to strive, if we are lucky enough to make it.

Personally, at this stage in life, I really didn't care if I made it or not. I was dark, dangerous, and depleted of any drive to live a "good life," if any life at all. There were so many close to me that died, that it gave me an intense numbness for the fear of death. I among many was the perfect definition of an undiagnosed post trauma victim. Besides my niece, I refused to go to Looney's/Cyle's, Sylvia's, Andre's, Wills, Sean, Paul, and Pookie's funeral. As a matter of fact, I wouldn't go to any other close friends or family members' funeral that died way before their time.

Everyone around never questioned me as to why I didn't go to their funeral services either. They inherently knew that I never wanted to see them in that way. Besides, I hadn't experienced a former church service since being at my Uncle Motley's church. Although when we were younger, one of my boy's mom would take us to her catholic church when they would have parties and retreats. There was nothing spiritual or religious about these experiences.

Our family had become a totally different family than the one that was expected from us when I was much younger. My mom was still brilliant, pretty, and held a polish about her, but she was however, the streets personified. "Nicky, we have to get ready and go and get you a suit for your grandfather's funeral. Oh, and by the way, you will be one of the pallbearers!" This funeral was not a choice. Not only would I be going but I was going to be involved.

I was sitting in my grandfather's house receiving instruction from my mother regarding my role in my grandfather's funeral "Nicky, it's hard to bury your parents." With a tone a bit above a whisper, my mom told me how she was named. She revealed in bereavement how her name was Carlyn not Carolyn, named after my grandfather Carl. I really saw how losing my grandfather had pained my mom even though she kept a very strong persona. My thoughts immediately rushed over all of my own memories I had with my grandfather.

You see, Carl was a charmingly refined man and unyielding in his expectations for his family. He never laughed if it wasn't funny nor scratched if he wasn't itching. However, he had a way to put you at ease if he was engaging you in conversation. Without him saying a word, you knew you were around someone who brought a larger presence into the room.

There was a quote that he kept over his desk in his particularly arranged mechanical shop in the basement of his immaculately kept home. It read, "You are the master of the unspoken word, but once it is spoken you become its slave." This quote stayed with me my entire life.

At the mall being fitted in a very expensive well-tailored Italian suit, I can recall how my mom spared no expenses to make sure that I was "appropriate" according to her family's standards. My mom's side of the family at that time only spent time with the educated, accomplished, and well off.

Though we grew up in two different worlds, my cousin and I were both admitting our disgust on how we all would be approaching adulthood soon and that we only found time to come together at our grandfather's funeral. On the surface we knew we were family and loved each other, but at heart we lived galaxies apart.

The open casket with the body of my grandfather laying in it was immediate trauma for our entire family. The solemn soliloquy of the organ along with the amber ambience of the dim lights set the somber tone. The obituary gave broad overviews of my grandfather's life regarding family, travels, and accomplishments then explained how he died and had gone on to be with the lord.

My grandmother Marie surviving my grandfather knew only my grandfather in marriage her entire adult life, and she was devastated. In all my life, this was the only time I seen my mother's side of the family express what I learned for the first time to be their deeper Christian roots and faith.

I later found out that my great grandfather was a

Presbyterian pastor in Pennsylvania. Honestly, I was proud of my mother's side of the family but found it difficult to relate to them. In my own head, I was deep in thought on how I was kin to this part of my family, but was turning out so very different, regardless of the same bloodline or the new tailored suit.

Making huge amounts of legal or illegal money, and or becoming the greatest rapper in the world were my goals in life, if I lived, was my thinking. With Post Traumatic Streets Disorder and a street-ran family, high educational goals was a far removed notion for us. You could literally tell that we had a totally different twenty four hours than my cousins' world.

Though I was barely going to school, I still read the Autobiography of Malcom X, Behold a Pale Horse, and was memorizing twenty five dictionary words a day from the SAT study cards I got from a girl I went to school with. Debbie, who was brilliant and used to make all A's, had already dropped out of school, knowing that I was right behind her. These were some of my craziest, darkest, deepest, and most painful years. I have vivid recollection of specific traumatic events, shifting the sails of my life, my family, and the people living around me forever.

# CHAPTER THREE

## *Entering the Fog*

**M**y skepticism of life having no bounds, I never believed in anything. I kind of naturally looked non-judgmentally at people who went to church, the mosque, or those holding any other religious affiliation. I gave them a second thought as much as I gave a second thought to anyone on the street or to death itself.

After feeling like I had already lived three lives and now just a few years from twenty, I never even thought that I would be alive this long. Everything that I had lived through, done, and seen, I knew that I didn't mind leaving

20

this earth for sure. I really didn't think I deserved to live.

Daily walking in this state of mind, I ran into my boy's mom, who hadn't seen me since I was very little. We were playing basketball in one of my friend's backyard. Ms. Jerri came straight out of the house and looked at me smiling and intense and said, "You've grown up so much, and God told me that you are going through a lot; God has so much for you to do." At this age, I had a very general knowledge as to the definition of God. However, with extreme respect for Ms. Jerri, I was intrigued that God would talk to me through her.

She talked to me for quite some time, and she was fully aware that my environment and lifestyle was contrary to the great life she was telling me that God had for me. I was trying to calculate the years of pain and seeming spiritual abandonment from the God who all of sudden showed interest in turning my entire life around.

I was really trying to piece together everything that she was telling me. She said "God had you go through all that you've been through and continue to go through so that he can use you to help change other young people's lives who will be going through their own trials and tribulations."

I was hesitant and respectful to all religions, and I didn't know enough to be able to deny or disagree with Ms. Jerri. She spoke to me in such a personal and uplifting way unlike I had ever been spoken to. My family had become decadent, I became evil, and so having someone telling me a different side; I wanted so much to believe her.

I needed to believe that I wasn't born to die early. I needed an answer as to why I lived in this environment and my family was turned out to the lifestyle of the streets. I needed to believe that I had a purpose bigger than the options presented to me.

After several encounters with Ms.Jerri, on this one particular happenstance, she invited me to a bible study in my neighbor's house where we were playing basketball. I told some of my boys and cousins that I was thinking about going in when it started. They all decided to hang out and went to her bible study with me.

Ms. Jerri had a son who was a few years older than me. His name was Mark and we called him Marky. Marky could have played basketball for the NBA easily. Nevertheless, he like most of us gave his youngest and greatest gifts to the streets. Ms. Jerri loved and pained for all the boys in the hood like we were all her sons.

That night she prayed like her personal familiarity combined with all of our experiences and pains were being lifted from us. My mind had never had the simple exercise in thinking that I could see me, the young people in my hood, or my family in a better state. She had emotionally expounded that Jesus Christ had called me from thousands of years ago and that he was still alive and wanted to live in me and help change my life and bring him glory. This is where several of us had b e c o m e "saved."

After clearly establishing that we were born into sin by reciting some passages in the book of Romans, it all seemed to make sense. This resonated with all of us who felt that we were so obviously "deep" in sin. Ms. Jerri quoted to all of us Romans the 10th Chapter and verses 8-10 KJV (8) "But what saith it? The word is nigh thee; even in thy mouth, and in thy heart,' that is, the word of faith, which we preach; (9) that if thou shalt confess with thy mouth the Lord Jesus, and shalt believe in thine heart that God hath raised him from the dead, thou shalt be saved.

(10) For with the heart man believeth unto righteousness; and with the mouth confession is made unto salvation." Hoping and believing that she was possibly giving me the answer to my life's ill fate, I confessed Jesus Christ as my personal Lord and Savior.

Ms. Jerri had a very charismatic personality with loads of passion. She taught with tears and joy as though she knew all of God's secrets. After that night, I viewed the world entirely different than I ever had. Never having a n y religion at all in my life, I thought that I found something that was revolutionary. I felt my life's journey was purposed and I was approaching the Bible like I had to understand all about it and know all I can about my Creator. I now thought that all I had to do is ask God and he would change my life, my family, and my people.

At one of the several Bible studies I had attended, and going through much struggle and temptation, Ms. Jerri read from the book of Romans chapter 8: verse 28 KJV (28) "And we know that all things work together for good to them that love God, to them who are the  called according to his purpose." The way she radically taught us our introduction to Christianity, made me want to be "the called according to his purpose." After all, God had me go through everything I was going through so that I could know him better and fulfil his purposes.

I literally hibernated for several months, reading the bible, going to bible studies, praying, and totally leaving the streets alone. Only those who were in the backyard playing basketball with me that day remotely had a clue as to the transformation I was experiencing. Girls, who I messed with sexually, thought that I was tripping when I wouldn't go. All my boys didn't know what to think about my new found  change, but they always respected me. They thought it was a miracle that I was no longer destructive and evil.

After several bible studies with Ms. Jerri, she finally broke down to us how we needed to receive the Holy Spirit. She read to us from the book of Acts (KJV), in chapter 2 verse 38: "Then Peter said unto them, Repent and be baptized every one of you in the name of Jesus for the remission of your sins, and ye shall receive the gift of the Holy Ghost."

She felt we were ready for the next step, and felt we were ready to be baptized and as she expressed it, "truly saved." She told us how her pastor was a young great man of God and that he was capable of teaching us the deeper things of God, as my appetite for scripture was now obviously deeper than weekly topical Bible lessons.

I had attended church for the very first time voluntarily. Everyone congregated at this building in the hood while the church was looking for another building. When I walked in, it had a strong positive vibe with good people. The church was full of young people, some from the hood, and some from the burbs. The music ranged from calming "praise" music to a new gospel contemporary style that I had never heard, without a choir.

Young people were actually playing the drums, guitars, base, and keyboards. They were singing and playing together. They were giving praises together, with intervals of lifted hands, very in tune with each other, while in their own zone.

Walking further into the church for the first time to take a seat, everyone was stopping and greeting me like they were really glad to see me even though they never saw me before. It was obvious that some of the guys there came out of the hood as well, but they immediately treated me, my cousins, and my boys like we were long lost brothers. Some of the girls or very young women dressed a bit revealing which I dismissed as some of them being on different levels in their faith. Amazed at the whole social dynamic and having  never experienced it before, I was totally dazed and did not know where in the fog I could be.

# CHAPTER FOUR
## *Where in the Fog*

Though I now had a little knowledge of prayer, scriptures, and salvation, I knew nothing at all about the deeper levels of church prodigals. I felt strongly that I needed salvation from the life I was living, and being in a "church" or a fellowship was a safe and neutral environment away from the world I lived in. The way everyone around me was getting strung out on drugs, locked up, or killed, out of nowhere came my new found church experience. I really felt that everyone I knew who was still out in the streets was just plain sleep on Jesus and that he was all they needed. This was my thinking and this became my life's path.

27

This really helped me grow faster as a Christian as I was observant, alert, and very respectful to everything I was now learning. I was absorbing it all in like a sponge. When someone was quoting a scripture I was reading and memorizing verses before and after the quoted verse or verses. After being baptized, Ms. Jerri would always remind me to "hide the word in your heart that you might not sin against him," her version of Psalms 119: 11.

I truly believed that I was saved just because I saw a great change in my life but was still told that I had to repent and be baptized. One Sunday, we went about two hours out of the city to our pastor's brother's rural church to be baptized. Before baptizing me, my pastor quoted Acts 2:38, "Then Peter said unto them, Repent, and b e baptized every one of you in the name of Jesus Christ for the remission of sins, and ye shall receive the gift of the Holy Ghost."

Coming out of the water with my white robe dripping wet, I knew everyone was waiting to see if I was truly saved. I set myself in a sincere mind contemplating the change I wanted in my life, and I just let my tongue go with what I was told were the utterances of God, "Ho ta ba la ta baba ha ta la laconda!" Something to that affect, all I knew was that everyone was excited for me for this level of spirituality. Whenever you attain (or are given) the "gift" of Holy Ghost with speaking in tongues, it is like having and wearing the true badge of salvation. This was the sign of having the truest most intimate relationship with God.

This was an entirely new life for me. We would have what we called "fellowships" at different church member's houses. I recall being at a fellowship at a young congregant's home who lived in a very nice suburban area. A lot of our church members were there and I walked in while several of them were in prayer and was speaking in "unknown tongues." We were taught that this was a sign of the Holy Spirit not only saving, but sanctifying, edifying, and interceding for your soul. Everyone present, who was committed and devout in their faith, was the same ones who seemed to speak in unknown tongues.

The church members who were in attendance were diverse with experiences or testimonies that made me feel that I wasn't alone in this life's struggle. This made me feel that attaining a righteous life was possible. I was very guarded now in my relationships with young women as I wanted to have a wife and please God with a family. So very different than how I was living or was raised.

No more violence, promiscuity, and debauchery, which I learned from scripture was causing the curses in my life. My displayed discipline from recreation to morals was now defined with intense purpose. My desire to read and understand scripture was more important to me than food.

Reading the Bible made me want to understand God, life, and death. I started reading everything. After almost two years of dropping out of school, one day I suited up and went straight back to the principal that expelled me, and told her that I wanted to come back to school.

Ms. Prater was in pure shock. She was very pretty with a Coke bottle shape, and I was the young misogynistic trouble making thug who was now coming and asking her for re-entry into school. She actually laughed at me and then soon noticed that I was not joking. I apologized for all the hell I raised and told her that my life was changed and that I needed to get back into school. I promised her that she could put me out if I violated one time and she certainly assured me that she would without my consultation.

Ms. Prater asked me question after question as she was both conflicted and inspired from the trouble I had caused in the recent past yet now demonstrated a totally positive changed energy. She was astonished and s h e could not believe that she was actually sitting down having a deep conversation with me about my changed life.

Eventually, she made me follow her to the school's counselor Mr. Brown's desk. He looked at me up and down, and had me sit with him so that he could process my re-entry. Suspicious with a smirk, Ms. Prater looking me up and down again while telling Mr. Brown, "Now look, I'm going vouch and believe his word that he's ready to come back into school and that he won't start no shit!"

Carlyn, Nate Baby, and Debbie couldn't believe that I had changed and was back in school. My whole hood was dumfounded. They all had my back and kept me spaced enough to focus on school. We always had drama and I was never "holier than thou" so everyone would still come and check in with me time to time from the hood.

I still had all types of opposition to prevent me from being successful in church or in school. However, I just wanted to know God. I wanted to know God so much that this mind frame provided a single-mindedness to facilitate a discipline to accomplish success in school, church, or whatever I set my mind to.

Every class that I took, I went and told the teachers that I was going to get A's in their class. They all having the same suspicion as Ms. Prater, smirked and also soon found out that I was not joking. I went to my economics teacher Mr. Beitz and handed him the first ten chapters of assignments from the economics class' text book. I did the same in my American government, algebra, sociology, and English classes. I took a Russian class and aced it.

I went to day school, night school and summer school trying to catch up from being so far behind. I went to teachers who taught typing and learned how to properly type, just in case my new found academic acumen went further. I would arrive before or stay after school just to learn how to type. I went from dropping out of school to now having a consistent 4.0 Grade Point Average.

Then there was that unbelievable moment, standing there behind the podium speaking to my classmates, ranked in the top ten of my class. Ms. Prater had me address my class at my commencement. Walking across that stage seeing the entire building going crazy in tears, because they knew my life and that it was a miracle to see me actually graduating. I realized at that moment that I had a natural gift to stand in front of an audience and speak.

This was an amazing feeling, seeing that I would have not even thought to imagine I would be graduating. Not only graduating though, but actually being in the top ten, and addressing my graduating class. Never envisioning that I would ever complete high school, I surpassed all of my own expectations considering now what college I wanted to attend.

"Giving all honor to God, for the change in my life," my new found viewpoint prodded me to possibly want to go to a bible college. Being excited in telling the pastor of the church I attended that I was considering going to a bible college, and I was seeking his guidance in my decision making process. I told him how I was considering Union College in New York, or Moody Bible Institute in Chicago. I told him that I learned that Moody named after Dwight Lyman Moody, was like the Harvard of bible colleges and that Union was a great school but it was considered to be very liberal.

Anticipating some profound wisdom from my pastor, he shocked me with his advice. He began to explain that he was well aware that I was gifted and he said that the Holy Spirit told him to tell me that "you don't need to go to school to learn the word; you have all you need right here at this ministry." He explained that he taught at a small bible college and that "God sometimes just wants you to sit up under your covering." He was assuming the position of the covering and I was to sit, of course.

Discerning the manipulation of him trying to persuade me against growing educationally and leaving his church, I explained to him that I now have the opportunity to go to any top bible college I wanted to and that I intended on doing so, regardless of his displeasure. It was as though he wasn't listening when he catatonically looked off and said, "The Holy Spirit can teach you all things." "Okay, then he can teach me all things in college," I thought. How he had handled my relationships in church and counselled me on my college decision caused me to never ever go to him again for any more personal advice.

# CHAPTER FIVE

## *Who in the Fog*

After careful thought and heavy consideration, I decided to go to Moody Bible Institute. Having often being in Chicago with family since an early age and still having a Midwest connection, this seemed to strongly influence my decision making. Matriculating into Moody Bible Institute (MBI) was an unbelievable accomplishment as I had heard how intense their curriculum was.

I was ecstatic to be able to learn the highest heights and the deepest depths of my new found faith at such a respected and renowned Christian college. I would listen

34

to Moody's nationwide radio station to hear Dr. Anthony Evans who I thought was one of the greatest expository preachers and that the whole world (especially Blacks) needed to hear him. I felt that Dr. Evans could really preach and was very biblical and highly respected as a Black theologian. I felt that he could use a bit more of the Holy Ghost but he was definitely much more versed scripturally and was overall more polished than my pastor was. I was ready to go to college to be polished in my faith just like him.

I envisioned Moody Bible Institute as a place where I would meet other Christians and that we were going to get together and change the entire world. I visited MBI when I went to Chicago earlier that summer, and there were hardly any students on campus. This was fine because I was just glad to see the school where I would be getting the deeper knowledge of scripture and my calling.

The school building structures were all mostly deep maroon or brown brick. The campus was larger than expected as it spanned a couple of Chicago city blocks. There was the famous Moody Christian Bookstore on the corner of Chicago Avenue and N. LaSalle Avenue. On top of the Book Store was the only women's dorm on campus called Houghton Hall. Directly behind H o u g h t o n Hall was the Alumni building which was before the largest men's dorm, named Culbertson Hall.

This dorm was on the corner of N. Wells and Chicago

Avenue. Wrapped around that corner was the Fitzwater hall one of the older classroom buildings. There were tunnels that led to each building. Cromwell Hall, which is one of the older yet stately buildings the school has, is where the world famous radio station WMBI had its broadcast.

Touring the entire campus complete with classrooms and the library, I was amazed to see that directly a block behind Dryer Hall (another men's dormitory) going west on Oak Street was where the NBA visiting teams would come and practice before playing the Chicago Bulls at Moody's newly built gymnasium, the Solheim Center.

After doing a full tour of the campus, I felt so official. I was about to truly be going to a world renowned Christian college. Not having to see the school from campus books or brochures any longer, I coveted the feeling of growth and accomplishment that I saw in the external structures of these buildings.

After the summer had passed, I was very eager to start college. Unlike what I had envisioned and anticipated, I was now beginning my college career at Moody Bible Institute. Totally different than my experience of touring the campus, this was the real deal.

When I first started attending MBI, it was a complete culture shock, no other way to put it. Out of the thousands of students, it was only a few Black students, and they looked suspect. When greeting the Black students, I would kind of nod my head at them as to say "what's up," and they would reply with a stiff lipped returned nod and say "hello." The international students were cool, but you could still feel the undertone racial tensions they assimilated into, although we all supposedly knew Jesus.

Getting acclimated in this new environment was a very bizarre adjustment. Although I had family in Chicago, I decided that I wanted to live on the campus to capture the full experience of my unexpected college life. I was assigned to the fifth floor of the Colby Hall building. Besides the international students who came across the seas to come to MBI, I believed that I had to have had the greatest culture shock on the campus.

Just think, I had just left the hood and all of a sudden I was now among hundreds of White students registering for classes at MBI's administration office. Students were talking about what professors and classes they were going to choose and avoid. They all seemed to know what to look for and expect and I, staring at my class electives, felt clueless.

I soon realized that there were only two Black professors. One of them was a full time professor and the other was an adjunct professor. At this point, I didn't know anyone nor did I know my best class options. I ended up choosing some of the most difficult classes and professors at the institute, I later learned.

What I initially found most shocking about Moody was that it was a very conservative institution in all aspects. If one never penetrated the interior of MBI, you wouldn't have a clue as to the divides I felt by such ultra-right conservatism. Up until this point, my interpretation of Christian doctrine and my expectations of this predominantly White Christian student body was disillusioning. My expectations and authentic experience at MBI was as far apart as south is from north.

Regardless to no Blacks in the administration, only two Black men on the educational faculty staff, and a very small number of Blacks in the student body, I realized that this institutions' focus was not Blacks. There was however, a small concentration of Black men working the janitorial staff and Black women working kitchen duties, none in leadership positions. Also, I quickly noticed a few Black women working in some admin capacities, i.e. phone switch boards, assisting in accounting, or secretarial jobs.

Moody Bible Institute prided itself on holding onto its traditional values, which I found to be out right offensive. More shocking than offensive to my theology was that though I knew MBI didn't endorse speaking in unknown tongues, I didn't know that they were actually down right against it. My thinking was that if you confessed Jesus Christ as your Lord and Saviour, received the gift of the Holy Ghost with speaking in tongues, then you were saved.

On the second floor of Fitzwater Hall, my apologetics professor taught that all Christians claiming to speak in unknown tongues are simply speaking in ecstatic psychological gibberish. Dr. McNickle showed us video footage of tele-evangelist, pastors, healers, and churches speaking in tongues and showed from an expert linguist perspective, that absolutely no language is being spoken by any of them in the footage. He explained that this was important because of what the bible says. He then taught explicitly, that the bible is every Christian's final authority.

He taught that Pentecostal or Charismatic churches started their tongues doctrine by taking the scripture out of context when they quoted the book of Acts chapter 2 verse 4 when it says, "And they were filled with the Holy Ghost, and began to speak with other tongues as the Spirit gave them utterance. He taught that the word tongue is the word "glossia" in the Greek and it meant languages.

Dr. McNickle pointed out in the book of Acts 2nd chapter, that those Christians were actually speaking in a real foreign language that was unknown to them. So basically, these Christians Jews were able to communicate in another foreigners or Gentiles native language around them without any knowledge of the languages themselves. Plainly, Dr. McNickle instructed, that this is not happening with people who so called speak in tongues today. He showed how the same experience is done by some Hindu sectors in India who hold totally different beliefs. He demonstrated how they were using ecstatic psychological gibberish and that it sounded just like tongues in the church.

Immediately I thought of my Christian experience and all the Christians I knew who spoke in tongues. I felt we were sincere in our "holy language," as I had learned to endearingly refer to it. This bust me over the head. He also showed how mostly all Charismatics or Pentecostals never really teach from scripture but more from their personal experiences and "revelations." He showed how this was "eisegesis," or plainly an abusive interpolation method which adds one's own interpretation to the biblical text. So imagine my frame of mind hearing this, it blew me away.

Now more than shocking but a disgraceful tradition I encountered was beyond offensive. Students framed it as college life carry-ons yet I felt it was disrespectful, humiliating, and bordering criminal. Before delving deep into the fog of curricula challenges, I learned that being a freshman in the Colby Hall dormitory, I was supposed to get "flag poled." This tradition almost brought the street out of me. This is where they would take the freshman in the middle of the night, tie them up to a courtyard lamp pole and would apply shaving cream all over their body and practically debase them. A form of hazing.

I let my entire fifth floor know that if they attempted to flag pole me, I would literally hurt whoever was involved.

My dorm mate next door to me, who played football as a line-backer in high school in Boca Raton, FL told me that he would get me out of bed and tie me up himself. I told him that if he tried, I would stab him until all of his blood leaked out of his body. Needless to say, I was never subjected to this offensive tradition.

Seeing that I entered Moody in 1990, I discovered that just a few years prior to my matriculation that Moody had just recently allowed Blacks to dorm with White students. Literally a few years earlier in the early 1980's this coeducational rooming together was not allowed. Moody being one of the highest respected authorities of Protestant Christianity and having this type of recent past was extremely disconcerting to me.

I soon found out through our daily chapel meetings that having a more Charismatic or Pentecostal background was also unwelcomed.

The student body met in the Torrey-Gray auditorium. It was a huge edifice with a capacity to hold about four thousand people with three level balconies. The red seats and interior walls were refined brown brick and exuded an inviting yet dim atmosphere. The chapel meetings were where the entire student body met daily as a requirement. The organ pipes small to large going from the stage all the way up the high ceiling. There were hymnals in the pews and words projected on the walls for every student to read and sing along.

41

The music was very rigid and stale. There seemed to be strong control and very little spirit in anything that was done in these services. Everything I learned before and how I learned it, was microscopically challenged from the very school culture I was now immersed in

Living in the dormitory was a great challenge. The building was older but well kept. There was a recreation hall on the 2nd floor. Even though Culbertson Hall was not gender co-ed, the women could come up to Culbertson Hall's second floor to watch movies in the theater, play the variety of games available, or go to the dorms café for popcorn, hot dogs, soda, and snacks.

On my dormitory's fifth floor on any given night, you could be informally inducted into the battle of philosophy conversations. Every student seemed to believe that if you are a Christian then you must be a part of the Republican Party and that you held Rush Limbaugh in the utmost regard. Honestly, these adherences seemed for the majority of these students to be more valued than their devotion to Christianity or to Christ. I would often tell these students that their allegiance to Rush Limbaugh, President George H.W. Bush, and the Republican Party is way deeper than their actual faith in Christ.

My refuge at MBI became my professor Dr. Rupert Simms, who was a great influence on me academically. My other havens of refuge were pastor Corby Bush, the former student and Afro Awareness Fellowship founder

Russell Knight, and current Afro Awareness Fellowship president Jah Ranu Menab. Any other Black professor, administrator, or employee seemed to be useless sounding boards to the realities of what this institution would get away with racially.

Like the unbelievable racist views held by the majority of the White administration and White Christian student body. Though they sterilized it as much is possible, the views held regarding the Black curse from the Old Testament is at the core on how they regard Black people or issues at MBI. Unfortunately, too many Black people in Christianity hold to this racist passage and commentary on Noah's sons, Shem, Japheth, and Ham. In Genesis 9:20-27, Noah curses Ham's son Canaan because Ham saw Noah gluttonously drunk. In the text, Shem (Mongolian, Asian, even Arab races) is blessed and Japheth (White race) was extremely blessed because neither he nor his brother looked at their father's nakedness.

According to multiple respected Evangelical scholars and commentaries, Ham's lineage represents Black people and Noah cursed Ham's seed or son's lineage the Canaanites. I have seen older commentaries that Moody still possesses in the annals of their library saying that Ham represents every Black person's cursed bloodline today. They can't deny their views even to this day, as they sure have not made any attempts to reverse the teachings of racist doctrine in their Evangelical circles.

You wouldn't believe the prevalent beliefs you might encounter on these dorm floors. I have had discussions with dorm mates on how Blacks are going through all that they are going through and have went through, because they worshipped idol gods in Africa, or because they pray to their ancestors. I can recall in Church history learning about how the late great pioneer frontiersman missionary David Livingston saved the savages. We learned how he was really unmatched in his reaching the multitudes of Africans and bringing them to Jesus and providing them a civilized faith.

In several of my classes you might hear how Jesus had this one "African guy" whose name was Simon help walk him to the cross. As if to pacify the one "Black guy" in class and practically saying, "Jesus loves you too pal, and there's a place for you in the kingdom!" In the classrooms or the chapel, Moody prides itself on being multicultural and above racism but White race was extremely important at MBI.

Moody Bubble Institute is what I un-affectionately refer to as my Alma Mata. The aloofness of Whiteness, and the arrogance of privilege is echoed through the halls and classrooms of MBI save a few. The donors and trustees are unapologetically pro-White, right wing conservative, dispensational, existential, evangelical, and republican.

When it comes to MBI's primary influence as one of the top academic Christian colleges in the nation and the world, it's Jesus and the GOP elephant and they breed that in the very fabric of the institution.

Most of the Black pastors in Chicago who went to Moody couldn't see this side of Moody because 99% of them went to the evening school program. This program was dedicated to the "Urban" or Black community primarily, and gave a sound yet easier, less rigorous academic regiment than day school. The atmosphere was more welcoming to urban Blacks in the evening program.

Academically, Moody would expose your weaknesses because it was a rigorous curriculum. My freshman course load was sixteen credits. I had to have a 5 to 10 page paper turned in almost every day as each class would require a paper a week it seemed. I was taking classes in Church history, Western civilization, sociology, English, intro apologetics, and hermeneutics.

For instance, one semester I took 19 credit hours. I had my four credit hour Greek course alone requiring nothing less than four hours of study and course work daily. My Greek professor Dr. Sower had us using over thirty declensions, translating from English to Greek, and back to English. I got all A's in this class but it costs me my time and mind.

My philosophy professor Dr. Foos demanded that we write long and frequent analysis from Socratic thought to the highest regarded philosophers, Soren Kierkegaard and

Friedrich Nietzsche. In my English class we dissected the book *A Severe Mercy* by Sheldon Vanauken who wrote about himself and his wife's relationship with scholar writer C.S. Lewis.

I loved my African American literature and sociology classes, both taught by Dr. Simms. He was a brilliant scholar and he spoke several languages. Dr. Simms holds a doctorate from Dallas Theological Seminary and from Loyola University in law. He was one of my most difficult professors but indeed by far, he was one my favorites.

I watched Dr. Simms go through so many politics at Moody trying to bring respect and dignity to Blacks within our learning environment. Dr. Joseph Stowell, MBI's president, and Dr. Charles Whaley the vice president were always trying to tame and regulate Dr. Simms, but they couldn't. Dr. Rupert Simms simply wanted Black students to be their absolute best academically.

As students, we would also be required to do the dreaded PCMs which was the acronym for Practical Christian Ministries that students had to do and received no academic credit for. Any form of intern ministry surrounding ones' strengths or gifts qualified for a PCM. I would always go to the Cabrini Green projects, one block away from the gold coast where Moody Bible

Institute's was located to tutor kids (my PCM). Strangely, I felt more normal in Cabrini than I did at Moody.

Cabrini Green in the 80's and 90's is considered to be one the nation's most notorious projects in Chicago. Some only know of Cabrini Green from the sitcom show Good Times or the movie Candy man. I knew of several other projects worse than Cabrini Green in Chicago, but felt that this one was pegged the worse because of its very close proximity to Chicago's gold coast.

Cabrini Green was a massive housing project that went all the way from Chicago Avenue on its south side all the way to Division Street on its north side. There was building after building after building. Going into the centre of Cabrini, as far as the eye could see, there were nothing but projects. There were churches, several stores, schools, and a police station directly inside the projects so that no one ever had to leave.

If you had no business in Cabrini, you did not feel welcomed to even drive through it. It was poverty stricken and massively overpopulated. There were different gang sects that controlled different buildings. To put it plainly, it looked down right intimidating and that does no justice to the actual fear one had if they had no business being there.

Every year in February, Moody Bible Institute would have Moody's Founder's week at the Moody Church on North

Avenue. The church and the school were two separate entities from the same founder Dwight Lyman Moody. Dwight L. Moody was the great evangelist who was a contemporary and close friend to President Abraham Lincoln. He was considered to be the Billy Graham or Charles Spurgeon of his day.

Moody's Church is a very large and beautiful edifice on Chicago's near north side off of Lake Shore Drive. The building makes MBI's large Torrey-Gray auditorium seem minuscule in comparison. The feel of the church however, was the same exact feeling and atmosphere that you would get from our daily chapel meetings in the Torrey-Gray auditorium.

MBI students were required to attend every day for that entire week of Founders Week. Founders' Week brought in some of the top Evangelical Ministers, Pastors, and theologians around the country and the world. I had the opportunity to get acquainted with some of these ministers from TV and radio faith programming. I remember my first Founders' week, there was the world famous Dr. Charles Stanley, Dr. Anthony Evans, Dr. David Jeremiah, Pastor Bill Hybels, and Dr. Ravi Zacharias on the program just to name a few.

My very first Founders Week at Moody, I watched the school raise multiple millions of dollars to help missionaries bring Russian students to America, yet they never even raised a thousand dollars to help Blacks in

Cabrini Green. The shame was that Cabrini Greene was only one block behind the school. Without needing to say, I was extremely conflicted with the great God I served and the great Christian college that He had me being prepared to do his work.

This was supposed to be a powerful week! Dynamic preaching, yet I truly wondered how we could put all these great men together and not overhaul all the conditions of any projects if we really wanted to. Realistically, I saw no difference from the time all these powerful men came to speak to us until the time they left.

I wasn't trying to be negative but watching this spiritual tragedy play out right before my very eyes, was hurtful. It was so consistent with all I had learned attending Moody. I being assured that I knew I was called by God, but seeing the obvious gross oversight of these spiritual men, it truly made me question who in the fog I really was.

# CHAPTER SIX
## *Well into the Fog*

Forging ahead in my faith and my developing ministry, I had a lot of young women who showed an interest in me during college and in the various churches I attended. No matter how attractive or interesting they were, or how interesting they thought that I was, I was already in a serious relationship before coming to Moody. I'd proposed to my girlfriend while in my first semester of college. My fiancé knew me, my family, and my life experiences so my connection with her was very deep.

Being certain of whom I wanted to be in a relationship with, and not wanting to displease God with immoral temptations, I ended up getting married in the second half of my freshman year. My fiancé grew up in the projects but she was raised in church. She could sing like an angel and she was respected as having a mature Christian foundation.

She was always praying for me and she seemed to naturally be prepared to be married to a minister. We could easily see that we would have a powerful relationship for God's kingdom. At our wedding she came down the aisle singing to me "if God be for us, who could be against us."

Anytime I had to go and preach, after I was introduced to the congregation, she would always sing before I spoke. I had no problem imagining the future with us. I would be a devoted and dynamic pastor and she would be right there beside me as an amazing first lady. Being around me in college, she also had received great insight on how to exegete any passage in the biblical text and how to teach or preach a proper homily.

We had pastors and first ladies wanting us to come and teach at their ministries. We were very young with so much responsibility. In my sophomore year, she had become pregnant with my eldest daughter. At that time, though we were a struggling young married couple, I would always tell my wife in rough times what Ms. Jerri use to tell me that "all things are working together for the good to them who love God and are called according to His' purpose."

I worked downtown about ten minutes from Moody and she actually started working for a professor at Moody's graduate school, right on campus. We had a small garden apartment on the near north side and it took us about fifteen minutes at tops to get to school and work. When our daughter was born, she stopped working and I took on the full financial responsibility of my family.

By the time I was a junior in college, I was already well into the fog. I was now a full time husband and father, and was practically a full time minister. I now had my firstborn and my second child with churches all over Chicago coveting my ministry gifts. I was working full time, in school full time with advance courses like homiletics, classical Greek, exegesis, advanced apologetics, and philosophy.

Having already served and helping ministries develop on Chicago's west side, I became the youngest elder minister at a fairly large church on Chicago's south side.

The church was located in what is famously known as the wild wild hundreds on Chicago's south side in Roseland. The building we held service in used to be a Catholic church. Besides the sanctuary building, the church's campus had a school, administration building, smaller chapel, and a rectory. The church's main worship building was the oldest part of the convent looking well over a hundred years old. Nonetheless, we put a lot of money into modernizing it and it was turned again into a beautiful contemporary structure.

I was the youth minister with my own building which was the youth and recreation building. We had a housing facility which eventually I and my young family resided in. The church living quarters was practical and rather nice. The building had been thoroughly renovated with new furniture, appliances, and was totally modernized.

The pastor and his wife were in their late thirties to early forties and he was a great speaker. His style wavered from expositional (preaching directly from the biblical text) to unapologetically topical (taking a passage and giving your thoughts on the text). Because I was from a charismatic church originally, I could tolerate some topical preaching but I was partial to expositional preaching.

On the outside of the church, you would expect to enter into a church styled much like a conservative Catholic church. When you entered nevertheless, the carpet was vibrant red and the pulpit was beautifully made of glass.

The facility was immaculate. The pastor could enter the stage from the back where the choir entered. There was a space to seat all of the musicians off to the right and left stage. The sound system was state of the art with microphones coming out of the ceiling over the choir.

Every Sunday the church was filled to capacity. The choir could sing with the best choirs in the nation. Some of the most talented gospel singers in Chicago graced the stage of this ministry. I would teach and have some of my professors or ministry friends come and teach. We had a fair amount of elderly people in our congregation but the overall demographic was a young, vibrant, and biblically sound charismatic church.

Like so many churches, the life backgrounds of the congregants were countlessly diverse. We had so many talented individuals who had strong desires to be all they could be for Christ. I brought in a lot of members from my school and the streets. We all looked at each other as family and we knew that we all had support for one another.

I was exhaustingly busy but I was so grateful. My family life seemed perfect, the Holy Spirit seemed to have total control, my grasp on theology was devout, and my ministry was blossoming. Having an influence on every young person from church, to those of various street extremes or gang affiliations was no coincidence, seeing that my own background was from the same environment as theirs. My ministry to existing or the "devout saints" was no issue because I was prepared to teach anyone who wanted to grow biblically and spiritually.

It felt like yesterday, while simultaneously an eternity away, when I myself needed to be ministered to from my own youthful nihilism. I was now preaching, teaching, training and counselling those who needed help. Who would have thought it?

I was approaching graduation from Moody Bible Institute. I was a committed family man. I was a seasoned and very active minister, an astute student academically and scripturally, and I touched so many lives, yet I was still exceptionally young in this fog with so much more distance to go.

# CHAPTER SEVEN

## *Anger at the Fog*

The choir was singing "Silver and Gold," and the entire service was high emotion with intense energy. Hands were raised and everyone was singing along with the choir expressing their personal devotion to Jesus, "I rather have Jesus than silver and gold." Afterward, we held general prayer and then it was time for me to come up and give today's sermon.

"The title of today's message is 'God's Unalterable Will.' And I'd like everyone to please open your bibles to the book of Romans to chapter 8:31-39." I explained how the Apostle Paul thoroughly and exhaustively wrote and

56

taught that absolutely nothing shall separate him from the love of Christ all the way to the end of chapter 8.

I taught as I had learned from Greek language scholars that when you read the original manuscripts, or read it in Greek, there are no dividing chapters and verses. Paul literally turned right around in the same breath at the beginning of Romans Chapter 9 and said that "For I could wish that I myself were accursed (eternally separated) from Christ for the sake of my brethren, my kinsmen according to the flesh (Jews)."

My message that day was that we as a people have been jailed, starved, persecuted, suffered nakedness, dangers, (punished with) weapons, just like Paul. Even more than that of Paul, we as a people have been enslaved, raped, murdered, whipped, dehumanized, bred, massacred, lynched, disenfranchised, discriminated against, and experimented on.

Saying look at how we have had genocide exercised on us as a people with the Tuskegee experiment with syphilis between the early 1930's to the early 1970's. Waking up the congregation's awareness, this message exposed a deeply covered similar operation. In this sermon that was exposing the World Health Organization's biological warfare against Blacks by injecting AIDS into Africans globally. Speaking about how it was being done by WHO under the guise of Smallpox vaccinations, a plan with beginnings back in the early 1960's. I didn't neglect the diabolical Planned Parenthood's Margaret Sanger, and the continued Eugenics experiments and genocide against Black people by Kaiser, Case Western Reserve, and the Cleveland Clinic.

Biblically bringing it back to how Paul said in Romans 8:38-39 that he was convinced that "Neither death nor life, neither angels nor demons, nor principalities, nor things present, nor things to come, nor height nor depth, nor any other created thing, will be able to separate us from the love of God, which is in Christ Jesus our Lord."

I scripturally demonstrated Paul's love for his people the Jews by proclaiming that nothing would separate him from the love of Christ. The great however was that he would have rather be eternally separated from Christ if his people could be saved. My message showed what love Paul had for his own people to make such a proclamation right there in scripture. At the same time showing that that is God's unalterable will for us. That is, that we should have such a love toward Christ, yes, but we must also have that kind of love toward our own people. "Against all of the impossible odds, we are still here. That's proof that we have to be vital to God's unalterable will collectively." I exclaimed.

Everyone present was on their feet because they were hungry for relevant discussions biblically broken down about the condition of Black people. They wanted to know "what says the Lord," to all these things we as a people are going through. When I was done, it was hard to get people out of the building that day; the energy was so high that people just wanted to share their excitement with what they had just heard.

My pastor had leaned heavily on me. During a certain time in his ministry, his personal life had prevented him from being in the  pulpit or church all together. He and his family were not on the best of terms. For all that we still know, it had nothing to do with his being immoral, but more to do with something psychological.

He would have me and a few other elders conduct the services in his absence for about a half a year. When he returned, he would still have me teach Wednesday night bible studies. Around the time of his return, if he were to teach on any given Wednesday the members would come out in a scattered number. On the contrary, when it was pre announced that I would be teaching, Wednesday night ended up looking like a Sunday morning church service.

This eventually did not sit well with pastor. He came to me the next week after I preached from Romans chapter 8 & 9, and told me that he listened to the message and that I was not teaching Christ centred  enough.

I rebutted that if I'm teaching bible centred and out of the Old Testament or some New Testament biblical passages of Pauline doctrine, I would have different applicable messages. I explained that we all preach messages that are biblical even if Christ wasn't the specific subject. His obvious angry reply back was that moving forward, as long as I preached in his church, that my messages needed to be more Christ centred, period.

Being a very young minister, I did all in my power not to rock the boat with him and to continue growing up under my pastor's ministry. However, my ministerial philosophy was simply developed into a mindset that if I was going to be ministering to Black people; I was going to uplift my people from the very opposite theological doctrines I had now learned at MBI to be offensive to me being Black.

My pastor went to an online bible college and took some evening classes at Moody Bible Institute to get his degree. He later went for his master's degree with a business emphasis. He had no idea of my totally different daytime educational experience at the same place he went to in the evening.

I began to see that his ministerial philosophy and views came from a modified type of training that catered to the busy Black full time pastor's schedule. None of these evening student pastors were empathetic to the racism Black day time students experienced. My pastor proved to be no exception.

Pastor was thorough on his knowledge of scripture and doctrine. He had never taken any classes about Black theology, history, or Black literature so this topic evaded him for the most part. It was really all about Jesus. He made sure that our ministry staff went through a very thorough ministry exam before he would license anyone for his ministry. To his observation, the ministry tests were too easy for me because of my level of learning but rigorous for mostly all of the other aspiring ministers. Nonetheless, he licensed me.

Besides being very busy everything seemed to be going well. Then out of nowhere, it seemed that I couldn't do anything right by pastor. All my messages seemed to resonate with the congregants and ministry staff but he seemed to not be impressed with anything that I taught, Christ centered or not.

Now, at every minister's meeting, it appeared that he wanted to take an indirect jab at me. On one specific meeting he had all of the elders and ministers vow to remain under his teaching, which I had no problem with. The problem that I had was when he said that God had placed him under the dispensation of Moses.

He told the entire staff that he was now going to be the spiritual father of the flock (church) and that we needed to submit to him like Israel submitted to Moses. We were supposed to signify this obedience by standing for prayer under his command. With all that I knew about scriptural exegesis and being doctrinally sound, I could not bring myself to stand and submit under any man requiring this blind type of allegiance. I was leery of his sudden need for submission and control.

Of course, he was observing who would stand and who would sit after giving such an edict. I was the only one sitting out of the entire ministry staff.

I remember the look he gave to me as I was unwilling to submit to him being under the "dispensation of Moses." He had a look that said, "Cool, I got something for you since you don't want to obey." This was a hurtful time, because I couldn't ever imagine that my pastor would ever succumb to this type of erred theological malpractice.

Mid that week, he requested a personal meeting with me. His office felt presidential. He had a stately oak wood desk with curtains that looked like they belong in the White house. The carpet was lush forest green, and the office furniture was straight out of a high ranking attorney's office.

I sat down across from him at his desk. Getting right to it, he told me that he wanted me to teach bible study for a couple of weeks and also teach my Sunday school classes. I asked him if he could see if some of the other elders could help me with the obligation of teaching as I had my finals approaching.

He plainly told me no, and said that if I wasn't ready for the obligation that he would just stop me from ministering altogether. I was appalled and confused at the statement. I told him that I have finals and that I was still going to be present within the ministry. He seemed both disagreeable with my response yet satisfied. I walked out of his office so far passed confused and angry.

As I was walking down the stairs from my pastor's office, I ran into Willie who was like a big brother to me. He would always be doing janitorial work in the church and security around the church's property. He was excited to see me as usual, and perceived that I was not my normal self, and saw that I wanted to explode. He asked me what happened and why I was so upset. I told him what the pastor had just said to me. He immediately became incensed because he saw how hurt I was.

That Wednesday, my pastor called a church meeting to replace what normally would be bible study. I had school finals and was taking a break from church that week. What I later heard that took place in this church meeting was dumbfounding.

I got a call from Sernard, my brother for life. I and Sernard were a Christian rap duo called GTU which was an acronym with multiple meanings. GTU meant Gifted to Uplift and Gutter most to the Upmost. Both of us rapped before coming to Christ so we were naturally using our gifts for Christ now that we were both saved.

When Sernard called me his voice was full of anger, disbelief, and hurt. He said that he was about to hurt our pastor. I asked him what happened. He described in broad sweeps that night's tragic meeting.

Sernard explained that when he first arrived at the church, there were hired security guards at the front entrance. He continued to tell me how our pastor said that I told him that I had quit the ministry, along with false statements of me desiring to take over his ministry. He said that our pastor lied on many other members in the church as well.

Sernard told me how our pastor had over half of the church members on a non-entry list held by the hired security. They were instructed to not let anyone on the list into the church that night. He said that I and m y wife's name were at the top of the list. There were so many others whose names I learned was on the list as well.

Sernard said that he got up and indignantly asked pastor how he could say some of the things he was saying, and our pastor reacted by going in on him about his spiritual walk. He told Sernard that he could leave too. I was infuriated with rage. I could not believe what I was hearing, and was becoming the more enraged the more I heard. The hurt in my brother's voice, the reality of what actually happened, and the many people's lives this pastor affected. Inwardly, I snapped.

I was already preparing myself for something crazy the day my pastor now wanted to lead the church under the dispensation of Moses. After having been shown so much love from him, it was beyond devastating for me. I was one of the few ministers who he would let come to his home with his family. He wanted me to teach his sons. He would always look out for me and my family. And for nothing, he betrayed me, my family, and so many others that I had developed lifelong relationships with.

Listening to Sernard tell me all of the details up until he left that night, I was becoming inwardly numb. I told him that I was going to see him later and hung up the phone to breathe. I received call after call, from the elders, the mothers of the church, to the members. Explaining to me and corroborating what Sernard had already told me.

This pastor had people's mortgages and hard earned money tied up in this ministry. He just shamelessly shut out the people from the church whom he cashed out on at the bank. No holds bar, with no holy restraint, that night my soul was screaming "What the fuck!" This changed the course of my life and so many others who became family to me over the several years we had all known each other.

Expecting way more of Christians, Christianity, and Christ from those bible studies back in the day with Ms. Jerri, I was done! I wanted nothing else to do with anything close to a church. Between Moody's inherent racism as ambassadors of Jesus, and these insecure controlling pastors ordained by Jesus, I hurriedly retreated far away from this dense thick fog.

# CHAPTER EIGHT

## *Reprieve from the Fog*

Riding shotgun in a brand new black 7 Series BMW doing over 80 miles an hour down a Beverly Hills 35 mph street zone. The world famous rapper DMX was at the wheel and I was bracing at every turn. X (is how DMX is also referred to) was playing and listening to my single Freaky on repeat. "Put that on a slow song, I know we wrong but we been doing this for so long, let's get it on. It's that passionate ecstasy, it's got us burning in hell but see it's heavenly. The seven sees ain't enough to put out the fire, we were true to our own but now we made a liar."

At this time, DMX would only listen to music from Michael Jackson and my single Freaky while he was driving. After successfully ditching his bodyguards, X and I drove to the Missions where the notorious 18th street Mexican neighborhood was. This is where X was getting his o l d school Chevy Impala worked on. They had already painted it white and were about to put a mural of his face on the hood.

My brother Sub introduced me to DMX. He was just finishing a concert in Los Angeles. Sub called me to come and meet him at one of Irvine California's luxury hotels. Sub came down and met me out in front of the hotel. Before we walked in he warned me that the lobby was flooded with Grape Street Crips from Watts. After X's concert, they followed him to his hotel. They were upset that his album was titled Flesh of my Flesh, Blood of my Blood and X's blood gang affiliations. I stayed locked and loaded so we confidently walked to the elevators, and then up we went to the penthouse floor.

At X's room door, down the luxuriously dimly lit hallway was his security guards Ben and Butler. Ben called X to the door for Sub. When he came to the door he had great energy. Sub told him I was his brother and that I was cold on the mic. X looked at me intense and said "dog, you look familiar?" I quickly looked back at him with sarcastic intensity and said to him, "dog, you look familiar too." He started laughing and called me a smart ass and he was considered family from that point on.

Determined to make my own way, I was very talented but humble. Entering into the penthouse, the room was unexpectedly filled with a lot of weed smoke and so many different energies. There in one room was a journalist and a camera crew from XXL magazine. Walking past another room filled with several racks of clothing for DMX was a room filled with several of the original Ruff Ridaz, and a few other artists on DMX's label. There was Drag On, some of D-Block, and Young Burg. There was PK, Swiss Beats, and Maurice Mann.

I was being introduced to everyone so fast. After smoking a few big fatties amongst each other, we immediately turned on a CD filled with instrumentals and began a Cypher (rapping with or against each other). After everyone went in, X looked right at me and said "TK, go ahead, give it to them!"

Without hesitation I spit, "If I could do magic, I'd take away the pains and the bad habits, wave a wand, to black hats for jack rabbits. Abracadabra, to all of my past sins, say rise again, to all of my dead friends, Hocus pocus, to all of these dope fiends, make clean and redeem their child hood dreams, say disappear to all of the effen fears, erase the tears from the strains of the hellish year, so rub the lantern, see the midst of the Genii, I'll clap my hands and grant the wish just like Houdini, escape the trials like of the Atlantic, I see the chains and the ropes but I won't panic…"

Before I finished, the entire cypher was stunned, and amped behind my bars. DMX was not only impressed but was inspired and did a very deep verse right behind me. After he was done, he came straight up to me and said that he was grateful to hear me and thought I had a place in Hiphop. Everyone else in the cypher immediately began telling me that I was hot, hands down. Throughout that evening, I thought of how privileged I was to develop a friendship and spend hours with one of the greatest Hiphop legends ever.

I stayed in touch with X and his management team, Maurice Mann and Christy Dash (maiden name Williams). As I was forming a relationship with Bloodline Records via Def Jam, I was dealing with the workings of my own record label that I established with none other than Antonio Gambino. The name alone could give clear insight into the type of environment I kept and the level of my mindset.

As the months past, I would run into DMX in different cities. On one occasion while X was back in Los Angeles, X, Tony, and myself were in discussion about me heading up the west coast division of Blood line Records. DMX would call me LMX (Light Man X), which was him expressing his respect for my talent. In my mind, I could see that I would be able to carry Bloodline Records on the west coast with the same level of impact that X exploded into the rap industry with.

I remember letting X know that I and Tony would be meeting him in Toronto, Canada. He was working on his movie Exit Wounds with Steven Seagal. When I landed at the Toronto Pearson International Airport, I had one of the most insulting experiences one could ever have. I and Tony were hand picked out of the line by Immigration authorities and were escorted to Immigration. They ran an extensive NCIC report on me and Tony and had us detained for over 8 hours.

At this point, I noticed that the only people they were hand picking out of the line were people who had color or non-white. They told me since we were coming into Toronto to conduct business with DMX that I needed to purchase a business permit. They said that I also had to pay temporary status because my jail record in the US would equal to a lot more time in the Providence of Canada. I was pissed. I told the officers that I have friends in high places who I could call in point 2 seconds. My friencs would love to bring the media to Pearson Airport and expose how Immigration is only pulling Blacks and Middle Eastern people out of the line.

Knowing how they pulled my background and Tony's whole family history from the Sadaghiani islands of Italy to New York, I was still raising hell about the treatment we received. The Immigration officer pleaded with me to calm down, so that he could try to work something out for me, but I was already snapping and was thoroughly outdone.

The Immigration officer left for a moment and w a s secretly talking with another officer. After his brief discussion, he came back with a reduced financial requirement. I had to calm myself to accept what became a 10 hour fiasco that led to a final agreement for entry into Toronto. They had me pay several hundred dollars for a temporary business stay, and several hundred for having an arrest record, which we both paid and were eventually let through.

When we finally got through, we got in a cab that was being driven by a Middle Eastern man who was wearing a turban. We told him the hotel we were going to, and began to drive off. As we drove for a few minutes, he said that he needed to be paid upfront and said if we didn't he was going to drop us off. I assured him that if he didn't drive me all the way to the hotel that his family would miss him. After cursing back and forth, he finally got us there. When we arrived at the hotel, we had this strong suspicion of being watched and followed.

That night we went to DMX's video shoot that was being directed by Hype Williams at the Toronto Maple Leafs' stadium. I told X what happened and he was upset for me but he found it to be extremely funny. He really took pleasure in poking fun at Tony, and would really be facetious with him to get under his skin in his funny kind of way. "Hey Tony… Why are you trying to bring the mob up here to Toronto?" X would say to Tony with a slight grin.

The next morning, Tony and I went out to grab some breakfast and I saw the front cover of the World Toronto Sun. I was stunned as I noticed that a major mob boss who was at odds with Tony's family had been executed. I showed it to Tony and we began to look around and noticed that we were being watched and followed like right out of *A Bronx Tale* movie.

Tony contacted his family, and they told us not to worry and to enjoy ourselves. When we got back to our hotel, the lobby was filled with agents trying to look inconspicuous. I told Tony that we know that we had nothing to do with what happened to the mob boss, so let's keep doing what we came to do and to let the agents watch us if they'd like.

I remember telling X what happened and that we were more than likely going to be under surveillance the whole stay in Toronto. X looked at me and basically said, welcome to his world.

We had good times in Toronto. I was there with my boy Eddie Griffin, his little brother Baby, along with Chung Li. Chung was first cousins with Jackie Chan and was a huge actor in the Chinese major motion picture industry. We hung out for a couple of months. Anthony Anderson was also on the set of Exit Wounds and was just like having a crazy family member around making everybody laugh. Between Eddie and Anthony, there was never a dull moment.

Viewing the large skyline of Toronto, Canada from the top floor penthouse suite of the Marriott Courtyard located on Towne Street was spectacular. Here as anywhere else, it was the tradition to have another cypher. My turn came around to spit amongst DMX, Young Burg, Sheek Louch, and some other notables. X always loved calling me out to spit in a cypher:

"Stand still niggaz, feel the world go round, cuz its six billion people, born in this world of evil, and every day as the world rotates, black babies born in love and niggaz die in hate, I set my eyes to the skies with my whys and maybes, as I cries to the stars of Abraham's cursed babies, going crazy, getting dizzy as this world keeps spinning, putting curses on my seeds while I keep on sinning, see I plead to Jehovah in the name of Jesus, my request ain't the best but I'm praying you free us, cuz work ain't honest but it pays the bills, and life ain't easy, nigga that's just real, so it's hard trying to figure where this nigga belongs, when the gravity pulls and the wind is strong, and life goes on and I gotta learn, that TK might die, so stop and feel the world turn."

After I would spit any verse, the cypher always felt inspired. There was always a great love that X and the

73

other MC's had for me and my lyrical gifts. I was all in on Bloodline records. I was working with Maurice Mann (DMX's road manager) and Christy Dash with Def Jam. We were solidifying discussions surrounding my music career and possibly heading up Bloodline West as I was now residing in Los Angeles. DMX was going through a lot personally and business wise, so unfortunately we never made this happen.

Over the course of a few years, my life had done a total 180 (360 as we like to call it). I was now in and out of the justice system, but felt that Hiphop was my saviour. Even when I became a Christian I felt Hiphop was important to reaching our youth in the Black culture, so I rapped as a Christian for outreach. At this point in life where I was this far into Hiphop, I was so disgruntled with the church and Christianity that my music had very little Christian influence as a body of work.

Now, my music and my personal life and choices resembled more on how I grew up over how I believed. My young Christian family was significantly altered negatively, and my wife and I had separated. Because I had never dealt professionally with the extreme hurt I experienced in the recent and distant past, I started to take it out on myself and my family. I literally became destructive to everyone and everything that I had built up.

I was definitely dealing with wanting to be successful, the psychological abuse from a pastor gone wild, and the undealt with sorted past I grew up with and was "saved" from. My wife at that time had to put up with my destructive behavior which included a gangster lifestyle, not excluding disrespectful unfaithfulness in our marriage.

My wife knew how I was reared but this was all rather new for my children. My two older children witnessed the transition from their father being a highly respected pastor to being a Hip-hop artist having run-ins with the law, and being the primary hurt of their mother. She was a faithful Christian and wife. She would have her family and friends have intercessory prayer sessions so that God would snatch me from my backslidden state. Narcissistically tearing my wife's heart to pieces, I was still strangely grateful just to as far away from the fog of Christianity as I could be.

# CHAPTER NINE

## *Return to the Fog*

Just finishing my last set, there were flashing lights and women rushing the stage. Back in my dressing room, I received the call that was bitter sweet. My wife had just had our third child, and I was out on a mini tour on the west coast. This was disturbing to our relationship because I was present in my first two children's birth but had missed my new son's birth. Though I was never violent to my wife, I was far past unkind to her. I was excited that I had another son but was disappointed with myself that I was not there supporting her and seeing him born as I did with my older two children.

I was just starting to peak in my career and was at the beginning of tasting fame. I was doing shows with some of the top names in Hollywood. The internal conflict spiritually and psychologically I was enduring was that the more successful I was becoming, the more my family life seemed to suffer.

At this time my wife moved back to Cleveland, Ohio. She resided on Cleveland's west side because she didn't want to have our three children in the hood on Cleveland's eastside where we grew up. As a mother and a wife, she held herself together during a tumultuous relationship with a belief that God will work it all out.

My belief in God was there, but I was very bitter toward Christians and church altogether. Christians that I had strong relationships with told me how hell bound I was, and that just further alienated me more than my last poisonous church experience.

I hadn't seen my family for months as I felt justified with chasing my dreams of taking over Hiphop. My wife was hoping that I was in a seasonal backslidden state. She separated with me and left me in California because she could no longer put up with me not being the family man she had once knew.

It was a heart wrenching experience for her seeing me once known and respected for being a redeemed didactic Bible expositor, to resorting back to the past I was once freed from. When she was giving birth to our son, I was out chasing my dreams and not living as a married man should. She felt abandoned, and I believed that I was taking my family to the "next level." This birth experience was not what she expected. Being in the delivery room and having our son without me there. That alone was not like she had known me, and she was distraught.

Though being extremely pained by my actions, she always viewed my struggles understandably and remained prayerful. Her latitude came mostly from her being aware first hand o f my sorted rearing and the abuse that I recently experienced in my Christian faith. After preaching on it for so many years, I now had become the prodigal son to her, and to those who knew me as a disciplined devout Christian and minister of the Christian faith.

I remember going to Cleveland to see my new son and children with punishing anticipation. When I came to the door of the house and saw my eldest two children, I was light headed and out of breath. The both of them rushed me like football line backers and we all came to instant tears of joy. I got the chance to see my newest son and I was almost out of my body in terms of the emotions of pain, excitement, and relief of holding him and realizing my transgressions of not being there with my family all along.

I had every intention on spending maybe a week or two with my family and then I was going back on the road.

Every day that I spent with my children and helping my wife take care of family responsibilities arose my first love and nature as a father and a husband. With all that we went through, I and my wife were reminiscent of our young love and naturally began to rekindle our relationship. We talked deeply about what was next for us, and I wasn't closed minded to trying to heal our broken family. Needless to say, I didn't get back on the road to pursue my music at this time.

Simplifying my life again, I took a job in Brooklyn, Ohio at a law firm to help support my family. I was still getting money from the streets as well and my wife didn't like to accept any street money from me. She tolerated me doing things she would have never tolerated before. This was partly because of her love for me, and partly due to her awareness of me still not being back "in the Lord." Mostly, she was just glad that I was living back under the same roof with her and my children.

It was autumn, the leaves on the ground and forty degree temperatures ushered in the fall season in Cleveland. Halloween was approaching and neither of us had agreed to have our children celebrating the most dreaded holiday for Christians.

While out running errands, I ran into one of my high school teachers and he had informed me that he was now pastoring at a church on Cleveland's eastside. He along with another pastor had helped me financially for a

79

semester or two towards my tuition at Moody Bible Institute. He informed me and my wife that his church was hosting a Hallelujah night. This was a children's gathering for trick or treating at church.

I didn't agree fully, but I told him that we would consider it because we hadn't determined what we would be doing for the kids for Halloween. He knew my entire family and had heard some of my journeys, and was grateful that I at least entertained the idea of going.

I talked it over with my wife and she knew how reluctant I was to even dare step into a church. I often said that the next time that I would be in a church would be at my funeral. Nevertheless, she knew just how to make it acceptable, "We're not actually going to a church service, so look at it as if you're just doing this for the kids."

I agreed to go, and from that point, I was conflicted with intense dread. I loved my former high school teacher as he was aware of a lot of my family's good and bad, and he was never judgmental of me or my upbringing. He was more like a dad that knew his son's nature.

Pulling up to the parking lot of the church, I was impressed with the size of the church's grounds. It had an obvious worship building with an additional L shaped building lined with classrooms. It was a former elementary school reformed into a church. I hadn't been inside of a church for some years at this point in my life. Inwardly, I felt awkward, as I had my guards up like a king who was protecting his kingdom.

I remember we all got out the car and walked through the front entrance. There was autumn themed decoration throughout the entire church. There were fun events for the children from the sanctuary to games orchestrated in each of the classrooms.

My former teacher, who was now a pastor, was elated to see that I actually came. He treated me like royalty and began introducing me to everyone. My wife was so joyful that she took the kids ahead to the different themes and left me with him to receive the grand tour of the church.

He showed me the entire facility and explained all the different ministries that were established or growing out of the church. I felt his excitement to just be able to show and tell me "what God was doing." He didn't neglect to share the opposition he was facing from some of the elders in his church either. I was appalled at the opposition, but not surprised as he was an installed pastor to a much older traditional Baptist church with many previous pastors.

After finally meeting back up with my family, he asked if I ever had intentions of getting my family back into church.

I told him that I didn't know if I would ever be quite ready for that ordeal. He smiled and didn't push it, but said that he would love to see it and didn't neglect to express that he could sure use my ministerial expertise in helping him develop his ministry.

I expressed gratitude for his invitation and his respect for my gifts, but I had already braced myself expecting such wooing back to God. With great understanding, he showed love to my family and he told me explicitly that his door was always open.

Knowing my Christian faith being the foundation and the only successful way to function in my family, it seemed that it was quite a divine time in space for me to re- evaluate my spiritual walk. Knowing that I was not living a Christ filled life even being back with my family, I really felt that we were not healed. My wife's prayers seemed to be penetrating my thoughts and spirit.

During this mental process, I became more open minded to what I needed to do to start the healing of my family. On my own, I began to secretly pray and read my Bible again. I withheld my cravings for smoking, drinking, and the entire lifestyle I was living. My wife didn't say anything but I knew that she took notice. After much consideration and prayer, I told my wife that we should go and visit my former teacher's church. My wife immediately, as they say in church, "cut a rug" with excitement.

I suited up for the first time that I was to attend a church in a very long time. Walking through the front door of the church, it felt a bit like Deja Vu. There was the red carpet, the congregants praising and lifting their hands, the familiar hymnals in the pews, and the extreme variant demographics of distracted youth and dedicated elderly. The drummer, the organist, and the choir director, directing the choir positioned behind the pastor's seat was all too evocative of my distant past.

My family and I were greeted by several of the ushers dressed in the traditional all white attire. The women dressed in missionary matching white skirts, jackets, and head pieces made them hard to distinguish from the ushers, save the red crosses on their head pieces. Seeing the choir sing, and everyone in church singing along with them, gave me immediate flash backs to what seemed to be another lifetime. I got smiles and welcomes from a few of the people that I met the night of the alternative Halloween church function.

Having such a diverse experience with so many different churches during my early ministry days, I was acquainted and recalled well the detailed protocols of a Baptist ministry. There was my former teacher seated center with two ministers seated on both sides of him directly behind the pulpit. He stood up with excitement when he got a glimpse of me and my family walking the aisle before we were seated.

It totally changed his entire countenance. I saw excitement and purpose all in his body language as he knew what his other ministers didn't have a clue. After the announcements, several more songs, and the alter call, he got up to preach and he had the church fired up and on their feet.

During the conclusion of his message, he asked for permission to acknowledge me, and with a nod I permitted him. He told the church some of my life's journeys and how grateful he was that I came to church that morning. He told the church that when I was younger, I raised a lot of hell in school, but God had put his hands on me and I graduated top ten in my class and went on to Moody Bible Institute. He told the congregation that if I were to get up right now that I could expound on the text in a way that he couldn't.

He further elaborated on the bible passage in Luke 15:11-32 concerning the prodigal son and was directly implying me in the message. His expounding on how God had brought out the robe, ring, shoes, and the fatted calf for his long lost son. "My son was dead, and is alive again!" It all resonated with me as I could see my life as being lost and how God was welcoming me back symbolically with this fatted calf of a welcomed return.

I was contemplatively ecstatic yet hesitant as I realized what the consequence of a recommitment to Christ would entail. No more music recording, tours, and the entire lifestyle that went along with that life. I was willing to do whatever it took to get my family back healthy, even if I felt that the church was a bitter experience that I had abandoned long ago.

At the end of his message and everyone now having a brief introduction of who I was, he called an alter call for prayer, salvation, and recommitment. My wife would not move as she wanted to make sure that she wasn't pushing me to make any decision one way or the other. After intense inward deliberation, I decided to get up and go and recommit my life back to Christ publically. My wife was in tears and overwhelmed with emotions as it was evident that she felt that all of her prayers were being answered.

After the service was over, I told my wife and my former teacher that I would really like to be low key in church and just quietly grow back in my faith. He conversely assured me that I would be preaching again soon, while half-heartedly obliging my request to be incognito. The desire I had to simplify my life, focus solely on my family, and please God, was bigger than being back in the fog of church and Christian onuses.

# CHAPTER TEN
## *Deeper in the Fog*

Every Sunday, it had become customary for my pastor to have me critique, customize, or give commentary to his homilies before he would preach. On Wednesday night bible studies, he would teach a passage, and after interacting with the rest of the students, he would lastly give me the floor for clean-up clarity. With all my life's experiences of being in front of people, I really appreciated having a limited presence in all the church services I attended.

Being aware of the problems that could arise in a church, my pastor began to make me privy to all the mischievous dealings happening within the ministry. He was up against a deacon board that was accustomed to controlling whatever pastor was installed into their church. The trustees were in cahoots with the deacons, so there was an entire resistance by the elders in the church. Perturbed by their actions, I was nowhere near discouraged.

My pastoral studies concentration at Moody Bible Institute served me well in helping my pastor combat these administrative challenges and situations. The more I helped him, the more his administration resisted. The more they resisted, the more I, his other ministers, and the congregation came to his aid. I truly had his back because I felt that I had already dealt with "ministries gone wild" in the past. The other ministers began to develop a strong respect for my knowledge and expertise.

People who were learning from my recommitment to Christ were in frenzy at the news. From Cleveland to Chicago, I was constantly bombarded with the phone calls of excitement of a large amount of people wanting to talk with me or see me now that I was back in church.

The excitement from everyone else fuelled my own. Approaching the summer, my pastor being very reluctant to push any ministerial responsibility on me asked me if I would be willing to run the vacation Bible school. He explained that it would be a paid position, and that would have to commit to it full time. He said that after vacation Bible school, he was assured that he could help me secure something full time at the church so that I could support my family.

After talking it over with my wife, I agreed to accept the position of being principle of the summer vacation Bible school. I remember sitting back in my office chair and thinking about how all of my life's escapades brought me to this point. I was highly respected by my staff, and was grateful to be where I felt I belonged. I was creating curriculums, giving wise instruction to my teaching staff, h u m b l y learning from those who were there before me, and most importantly, being loved by the students who attended. That made it all worth it.

My wife was excited, my children attended the vacation Bible school, and I felt that we went through all that we went through to come back together stronger than ever in Christ. During the summer, my pastor finally got me to agree to teach a few bible studies and preach a Sunday or two. Patient and humble, I was in no rush to be the great "young minister" I once was.

I was back immersed into heavy Bible study and doctrine. After that summer my pastor had me regularly helping him with preaching, teaching, and administration. Before I knew it, I felt that I had picked up right where I left off years ago. For all who knew me, they were grateful that I had once again conquered Satan's attempt to take me away from Christ and the ministry.

My wife and I decided to go back and visit Chicago where we spent the majority of our married life and where both of our older children were born. We were excited to be back in Chicago together and were fused with so many memories of our young marriage. We drove around the city and noticed so many changes.

It was to no surprise that several people in Chicago strongly desired my return to the city. All of the Christians who had attended the church that we all seen self-destruct, were scattered in a few other ministries throughout the south side of Chicago. One of the elders had a ministry primarily filled with remnants of our past church. He said that he had been praying for me consistently for years and would be honored to have me come and preach at his church.

As I pulled up to the church, there stood an all-white building with a tall steeple in the southwest suburb of Chicago. It was about the fifth of the size of our old church. When I entered, I saw a packed church with so many familiar faces with the exception of a few. The children seemed to have all grown up, and the teenagers I used to teach were now all young adults. Immediately when they saw me, the church erupted into tears and rejoicing. It was quite overwhelming for me and my family.

I could barely preach that day as there was an intense energy returned at my every word. It was miraculous for them and astonishingly ethereal for me. We were marvelled at the odds of our reuniting in such dramatic form.

On this trip, we had several meetings with old friends who felt like long lost family. They asked in detail about my life experiences and wanted to know if I had intentions to permanently residing in Cleveland. Quite frankly at that juncture in life, I had never thought about it. Seeing that I hadn't lived in Cleveland since being a teenager, and now residing back in Cleveland for over a year, I hadn't giving any thought towards where I would be permanently residing. Besides me being back in church, and missing a few of my love ones who weren't Christian at all, my affinity for living in Cleveland was very small.

Our Chicago family and friends asked if I considered coming back to Chicago to minister and help heal all the people who were influenced under my early years in ministry. These conversations were definitely something for me and my wife to think about. It was apparent that our children missed their city of birth and early rearing.

Returning back to Cleveland and multiple trips back to Chicago, we deliberated the pros and cons of returning to ministry in Chicago. I was offered an installation opportunity in the projects of Cleveland called Garden Valley not far from where I grew up. I went and visited the ministry a few times and was seriously contemplating their offer to take a pastorate there. The administration at that church was courting me heavily. My pastor said that he thought that I would fit well in that ministry, but I was not certain that I would personally.

I eventually declined the offer, but told my pastor that I definitely believed that my natural abilities were moving me to pastor, but I wasn't sure where. I told him that I was wrestling with going back to Chicago and starting a ministry from scratch. He explained to me the pros and cons of starting a ministry verses being installed into one. He said when you're installed you have your salary already worked out, but you still have to deal with what he was going through. He said there's a struggle to start a ministry but understood that I had plenty of support in Chicago. He assured me that he would be prayerful and that he would support me whichever way I decided to go.

I prayed, consulted with my wife and pastor, and my spiritual support in Chicago on which direction I should take. All signs seemed to point to Chicago. As a family, I and my wife thought that it was the Lord's will for me to start up my own ministry in Chicago.

Finally, I told my pastor that I believed going back to Chicago was the will of the Lord for me. My pastor graciously replied that if that is what I believed God's will was for me, that we needed to work on my ordination service right away. He was hoping to ordain me and install me in a ministry in Cleveland, but stated that he wouldn't be selfish against God's will.

My ordination service was a very big ordeal. Leading up to it, I had several experienced pastors in Cleveland meeting with me to provide the best wisdom for ministry that they could impart. There were family and friends all over Cleveland preparing to attend, and a great number of people coming in from Chicago. This was a monumental event to take place on September 11th 2005. "You are invited to the charge of ministry for Nathaniel McCrary II," read the invitations with my government name.

The night of my ordination the sanctuary was packed with church members and visitors. Visitors came from all across the city of Cleveland, and Chicago. The ordination service was scheduled to come right after my catechism.

That night, I was catechized from a panel of five pastors who presented me with 100 questions of Christian doctrine.

There were two doctors of divinity on the panel, and all were graduates of theological colleges. One of the pastor panelists for my catechism was a Messianic Jew and theologian. Out of all 100 questions asked of me, I was the first to their knowledge who had ever passed 100 percent of these catechizing questions.

After successfully passing my catechism, I went into a

packed sanctuary filled with great anticipation. When I came into the assembly, my pastor told everyone that I was the first that he had ever seen ace a catechism with flying colors the way I did. All present in the audience rejoiced at the news.

Right before ordaining me, pastor began hyping up the audience by saying, "Today is September the 11th and this is the day that we now get revenge on the enemy. This ordination is symbolic of us defeating the terroristic kingdom of Satan." He had this way of rallying everyone in the crowd. After quieting the full panel of pastors and the packed church, my pastor commenced with the ordination.

Beginning he said, "man of God," then quoted 2 Timothy 4:1, 2 saying "I charge thee therefore before God, and the Lord Jesus Christ, who shall judge the quick and the dead at his appearing and his kingdom. Preach the word, be instant in season, out of season, reprove, rebuke, exhort with all longsuffering and doctrine."

He also quoted 1 Peter 5: 2-4, "Feed the flock of God which is among you, taking the oversight thereof, not by constraint, but willingly, not for filthy lucre, but of a ready mind: Neither of being lords over God's heritage, but being ensamples to the flock. And when the chief Shepherd shall appear, ye shall receive a crown of glory that fadeth not away."

He concluded his message and charge to me by stating that "this service was to certify that after a satisfactory statement of his Christian experience, his call to the ministry, and views of bible doctrine, Minister Nathaniel McCrary II is now publically ordained to the gospel ministry. The Council assisting in the examination was composed of five messengers, representing five churches." Immediately, the congregation stood up full of joy and clapped endlessly it seemed.

Afterward, I was giving a robe, bible, and other gifts expressing gratitude for my acceptance of the call to ministry. There was high energy that night as everyone present came around to greet me and give me personal words from their heart. Now being deeper in the fog, it was an exciting moment in my Christian walk.

# CHAPTER ELEVEN

## *Even Deeper in the Fog*

Remembering Chicago from being young, it had become a totally different city than the 80's to the 90's. Back then and even further back, Chicago south and west sides were notorious. I have lost so many people who I love and miss. It was much more violent then, but strangely much more structured, particularly before they locked up all of the major street organization leaders as what most refer to as gangs.

Street life or violence was not all encompassing as you could see a different side with some Blacks who were doing a lot better than most. Hyde Park is on Chicago's

95

south side, now famously known as President Obama's neighborhood. It was a strong presence of renaissance Blacks who were teachers, lawyers, business owners, doctors, intellectuals, spiritualist, philosophers, and artist, who would convene with all of their differences, and without violence or trepidation.

There was the courtyard off 53rd. Street named Harper Court. This is where young and older men would be battling philosophy of life over chess games on the many chess stoned engraved 64 squared tables. At any moment, you might hear an old man curse out a young man, or a young man's strong protest, but no violence.

Till this day, 53rd. Street is busy with foot and car traffic, with a strong holistic community, a co-op, and stores. Living alongside and surrounded by Indian, Italian, and Soul food restaurants. Although I have seen it go through so many changes, you can still see a skeleton of what it used to be. Some of my favorite restaurants are no longer there, and I've yet to patronize most of the new ones.

There are shops and restaurants right next to each other and the hustle and bustle seems to capture many decades time past; you can just feel the history viewing the homes, condos, and tall apartment buildings. This could be easily said of all Chicago, or most cities for that fact, but the feel of Hyde Park has an exclusive renaissance energy in its social flow and architecture.

For anyone who has ever gone to Chicago, it is one of the most beautiful cities in America with an amazing skyline. There are so many different dimensions to the city. Up north, there's shop after shop, restaurant after restaurant, like one hundred Hyde Parks. Near west and near south from downtown, block to block, neighborhood to neighborhood has a thousand different stories they tell.

Excited to move back as it was home to us, and finding o u r new house, we set our minds for full time ministry. We got our house all packed up in Cleveland, and we made the move back to the south side of Chicago. The city had changed so much from the gentrification taking place all over the roughest neighborhoods in Chicago from before I was born to the 90's.

All the projects that were intimidating to look at or be in the neighbourhoods of in the 90's were now all demolished, and newly upscaled communities were being built. We moved a little south of the University of Chicago in the 20th ward, in a neighborhood called Woodlawn. This is where we immediately began to establish our new church.

We already had a little over 10 people who we had known for years and were mature Christians and committed to helping us launch the ministry. Feeling personally inspired to create a haven for hurting souls and running it by my new members, we all decided on the name Ark Ministries. The mission statement of our ministry was "Taking nonreligious people and making mature Christ followers." The ministry was very biblical in our approach, yet very non-traditional. We had strong Bible students and very educated members, to people who were fresh off the streets and who had very little knowledge of scripture.

Seeing that we were a new and developing ministry, we initially held our services in our home or in other church member's homes. We had leadership meetings often as we had to establish our ministry and file as a 501c3 (non-profit tax exemption) with the Secretary of State, Jesse White's office. We all had strong sense of purpose, and were very focused on having a ministry that was cutting edge and revolutionary.

The entire process was exciting and fulfilling as we believed our approach would help bring more people into God's kingdom. We started to grow beyond being able to hold church services in houses, so we eventually needed more space. We began holding our Wednesday night bible studies at a community center on the low end of Chicago's south side. Our Sunday services were now being held at a hotel's hall out in a Chicago's south side suburb.

It was not uncustomary for my entire church to join me in fellowshipping at other church's Sunday services as I was invited a lot to speak at multiple ministries throughout the city. There was an excitement to our young ministry. The word had gotten around to those who knew I was back in the city, from those who were now in other ministries and who hadn't been back in church since our younger years. I had learned of all the people who left church altogether as a result of feeling disenchanted from the ministry that we all had gotten hurt by years ago.

I was invited to be on a panel to debate Christianity versus Islam. The pastor who hosted the event had a nice size ministry on Chicago's far south side. I had preached at his ministry several times and hosted multiple seminars. He wanted me to come in and shut the traditional Islamic and the Nation of Islam down doctrinally. He knew that I was gifted in handling scripture and wanted me to lay-in on Christianity's arch opponents. The room had Christians and Muslims in anticipation to see who would win the battle of the faiths regarding the provability of their truths and doctrine.

On the panel were myself, a traditional Islamic sister, and a few known ministers from the Nation of Islam. They all spoke their positions and were all very passionate as to why they were on the side of truth. I remember taking a breath and then explaining to my Muslim brothers and sister that the Qur'an advised them that they must be respectful of the "People of the Book (Jews and Christians).

Quoting directly from the Qur'an to them I said, "Today all good things have been made lawful for you. And the food of those given the Book is also lawful for you and your food is lawful for them. So are chaste women from among the believers and chaste women of those given the Book before you, once you have given them their dowries in marriage, not in fornication or taking them as lovers. But as for anyone who disbelieve, his actions will come to nothing, and in the hereafter, he will be among the losers. (Surat al-Mai'da: 5).

The shock that was on the faces of the Muslim brothers and sisters was revealing. They expected me to stick strictly and solely to biblical references and normal Christian pastoral rhetoric. I explained to all present, that if I were to walk outside and get shot, and there was only a Muslim doctor who prayed to Allah to help save me with his medical skills, I would definitely welcome that over a thousand prayers from Christians. I explained to everyone in the room that the order of any of these discussions are futile unless they end with mutual love that represents our faith, and mutual respect based on the tenets of both of our faiths.

The pastor, who orchestrated what he was hoping to be a powerful ambush on the Islamic brothers and sisters, was enlightened, but yet was in complete shock. Expecting me to use my skill of apologetic swordsmanship and mercilessly slay my opponents, he discovered I believe for the first time of what it truly means to love unconditionally. From that point moving forward in my ministry, I was greatly loved and appreciated by both Christians, Muslims, my own members, and the NOI.

Above and beyond my ministerial duties, I worked in the community in different capacities. One of our church members had a sister named Karen Hicks. Karen asked me to help her with helping Black entrepreneurs keep their business in Chicago. There were a good number of Blacks business owners making pretty good money providing transportation to special-needs adults to their adult day care centres and back to their nursing home facilities.

Most of the adult day cares were owned by very well-known Jewish families in Chicago. They not only owned the day cares and nursing facilities, they also owned the medical supplies used by the facilities.

Seeing that there were Blacks, even some becoming millionaires through these transportation services, there were several Jewish families wanting to own and control the transportation businesses as well. Karen helped form and lead the Illinois Medical Transportation Association, including mostly all of the Black owned transportation businesses in Chicago and surrounding suburbs.

I became the spokesperson for IMTA. We went down state to Springfield and raised hell at the capitol. We consulted with Myrna Mazur of The Mazur Group, and I became the registered agent from the state (lobbyist for Illinois) for the IMTA. We were up against more than a mob monopolizing a business, but something that was later discovered controlled by politics and race. The Nation of Islam showed up to every engagement in this process to ensure that I was protected against some historically dangerous families.

Having become family with my Nation of Islam brothers and sisters, The Honorable Minister Louis Farrakhan gave command to make sure that I was detailed whenever I spoke anywhere moving forward. At this point, I would teach in my church and the mosque. I was the only Christian pastor who had ever spoken or preached in the mosque. My ministry would sometimes have more Muslim brothers and sisters than Christians. I loved my NOI brothers and sisters and they loved and protected me.

One day, my wife and I ran into a friend we once knew from our old church. She told me that she just found out that the pastor of the church she was now attending had molested her niece. This pastor lived directly across the street from her. I knew the mayor and the commissioner in this south suburb where she and this paedophile lived. The next day I informed the mayor and police commissioner of what I had learned and that I along with my force of brothers was going to pay him a visit.

The brothers surrounded the house and I and a few of us went to the door. There is a certain FOI (Fruit of Islam) way to enter a door in these scenarios that are not for publishing. In short, we addressed this brother and his transgressions, unfortunately with his wife now fully aware that she was spiritually following and more sadly married to a worthless paedophile.

As a pastor, I felt it was not only my obligation to serve people in ministry with just the offering of spiritual salvation, but that I must also work in bringing physical salvation. A spiritual person, biblical in teaching, a lover of all knowledge, and now walked with the presence of my grandfather Carl.

Being rational, moral, logical, ethical, and judicial, was my ministry style. Just from how I was raised, I loved hard but I didn't tolerate anyone's mess. I believed the Holy Spirit had a different kind of work for me, as I took my sheep (church members) as family who would always have the protection of their shepherd.

My spirit transferred over to those who followed me in ministry. My soon to be ordained ministers were biblically sharp and were equally hungry to heal our people. Together, we foresaw a ministry that would address all of our issues as Blacks living on the south side of Chicago, and show how Christ's kingdom and Christ's words was the answer for all of our struggles. As the ministry was beginning to grow, we all had no idea how deep in the fog we actually were.

# CHAPTER TWELVE

## *Exiting the Fog*

One day, my wife ran frantically into our bedroom and said, "You better talk to your daughter right now before I kill her!" "What happened," I asked. She explained with short breathes that my daughter had told her that she no longer believed in the Virgin Birth, or ever really believed in it. My wife was distraught that our first born looked at the Immaculate Conception as a religious myth.

Our daughter was home-schooled and created her own language at the age of nine. It was a very amateur attempt linguistically, but it definitely exposed the creative and analytical mind of a young intellectual. She was much ahead of her time as she was exposed to books that most adults hadn't read. After reading *The Destruction of Black Civilization* by Chancellor Williams, she had such a grasp on the current conditions of Black people in America and the subject of African people globally, and for this I was beyond impressed and extremely proud.

Knowing my daughter's intellectual prowess regarding history and religion, I was reluctant yet reassuring to my wife that I would make sure to talk to her and set her straight. I was more verbally confident than actual because I had no clue why my daughter was so buoyantly firm and vocal that the Immaculate Conception was a fairytale.

Having a look of expectancy that I would be coming to talk with her after shocking her mom into a close heart attack, she calmly and invitingly understood me sitting by her and preparing my inquiry into her recent declarations. Her face was serene and steady as she responded to my question, "you do realize that the Immaculate Conception is one the most essential doctrines in the Christian faith, don't you?" "I do," she responded without hesitation.

Her firm stoic response while demonstrating knowledge of handling an explosive dynamite of claims was unnerving t o me. Trying not to show any clue of mental unravel at her body language, I exuded the image of confidence in my calm questioning. "What made you question the most significant doctrine to Christ's divine nature?" She began to smile, and said, "Dad. This just doesn't make sense." While showing the appearance of supreme appeal, she said, "the more that I read, the more this just doesn't make any sense to me."

Exegetically with my very best biblical defense of doctrine, I explained to my daughter the importance of the Virgin Birth. She had me pulling out the book *Evidence That Demands a Verdict* by Dr. Josh McDowell. I was showing her Henry Thiessens' book *Systematic Theology*, explaining theologically the doctrine of Christology and the Virgin Birth. I explained to her my testimony and how it was evidence that Christ had to be real because of the change in my life.

She seemed to listen attentively, yet tolerantly. She appeared to have empathy toward my passion for Christ, but like one who's grateful for the person but not emotionally invested in the experience, she was unmoved deep within. I was stunned. I loved my daughter and taught her to think critically since she was a baby. I would not withhold her from her own deductions after teaching her to be impartial to the evidence on whatever she was studying or examining academically.

After realizing that there was no getting through to her, I told her that I would never try to force her to believe anything that she didn't want to believe. I expressed that I loved her regardless, and that she is entitled to come to her own conclusions in life. Knowing that she had infuriated and devastated her mom, she seemed grateful to still have the support of her father whom she knew she had disappointed with her statements.

I took what felt like an eternal walk down the hall, heading back to our bedroom, replaying our conversation. Walking slowly to the bedroom door, contemplating on how I was going to tell her mom. My wife was in anticipation of the results of our talk. Asking before I could barely shut the door after entering the room, she verbally shot off "How did it go?" and "What did she say?" "I know she ain't still on that drive by mess, is she?" Her questions immediately let me know that this was going to be a difficult realization for her and our family.

I had to sit down with her through her painful tears and explain that our little girl did not believe what we believe. She was wondering what happened. Immediately, she thought that she must have done something terribly wrong by having her first born denounce a major tenet of our faith. I reassured her that it was just a season that our daughter was going through and that she would return.

I was a pastor with an unbelieving child. Subconscientiously, moving forward in ministry, I made it my business to make sure that my church knew apologetics and hermeneutics to guard against disbelief. I never exposed my daughter's views, but I was always trying to present the Word in such a way that my daughter would return to the faith we gave her. We felt she came to church because she had to, and she was okay with it because we were her parents and we were in ministry. She never acted out or became disrespectful. She was always alert, yet always aloof while in church.

When it came to the ministers in Ark Ministries, we prided ourselves on having strong moral and spiritual lives, and were exquisite students of the scriptures. In the back of my mind, I wanted to make sure that no one else's child would be lost to disbelief. I had the ministers in the ministry study church history, hermeneutics (the art and science of interpretation), apologetics (the defense of the faith), and homiletics to reinforce expository teaching and preaching.

There was one ministers' meeting in particular; we had the men and the women ministers discussing passages from Pauline doctrine. We were looking in the book of I Timothy 2:11-15, after describing how a woman's attire should be, starting in verse 8 Paul wrote "(11) a woman should learn in quietness and full submission. (12) I do not permit a woman to teach or to assume authority over a man; she must be quiet. (13) For Adam was formed first, then Eve. (14) And Adam was not the one deceived; it was the woman who was deceived and became a sinner. (15) But women will be saved through childbearing—if they continue in faith, love and holiness with propriety."

I explained some of the most conservative to the most liberal commentary on these verses and that they all are controversial throughout Christian theological circles. Unfortunately, as we were all wanting to be pleasing to the Holy Spirit and not found using eisegesis (not adding our own or a cultural interpretation or biases to the text), we were more unnerved by this meeting than having peace regarding the subjects discussed. We wanted to have a ministry with woman leadership but were confronted with our own commitment to be biblically sound.

Notwithstanding, in that meeting now turned into a ministers' bible study, another troubling passage in Paul's letter to Timothy was on the table for discussion. I had some very culturally conscience ministers who were concerned with Paul's verse in I Timothy 6: 1-3.

The verses read "Let as many servants as are under the yoke count their own masters worthy of all honour, that the name of God and his doctrine be not blasphemed. (2) And they that have believing masters let them not despise them, because they are brethren; but rather do them service, because they are faithful and beloved, partakers of the benefit. These things teach and exhort. (3) If any men teach otherwise and consent not to wholesome words, even the words of our Lord Jesus Christ, and to the doctrine which is according to godliness."

I remember this meeting because it had spawned a new and uneasy direction for our now growing ministry. We had spent the following weeks and past month concentrating on some of the most controversial scriptures in the attempt to settle them once and for all as they came up in our ministry.

I told the ministers that we would all began to do a group study on various topics. We would collectively tackle subjects like how the scriptures were canonized, the Council of Nicea, and textual criticism according to Christian theology and history.

*** On your mark, get set, go! ***

We all began looking at canonization first, and this opened up so many cans of worms that were unimaginable to me and the entire ministry staff. I became reacquainted with subject matter we were introduced to at Moody Bible Institute. The difference now was, I was doing it from an independence of recommended sources and the required readings and filters of a professor. We began looking at written scholarship on the Q, L, M and X manuscripts that gave us our currently written Holy Scriptures.

The more we read collectively, the more questions we all had internally and individually. Some of the ministers on staff said they felt like they needed to stop reading challenging scholarship as it was disrupting to their faith. We examined without satisfying answers on the exhort Greek & Latin manuscripts being authoritative with so many errors, contradictions and incompletions. The scholarly explanation of how the scriptures coming to doctrinal fruition was a lot more messy and a lot less lofty on how we were all taught traditionally.

For example, I prided myself on how well read and trained I was on Koine (classical or ancient) Greek. I thought that I was really learning how to read God's word in color when I learned how to translate from Greek to English and from English to Greek. I was dumfounded to find out that in 1705 that Dr. John Mill (linguist from Oxford University) translated the first Greek New Testament from Latin. He was only allowed to create this Greek New Testament from one hundred of the 5,700 manuscripts available.

John Mills giving commentary on his work of translation said that he noted over 30,000 discrepancies while creating this first Greek Novum Testamentum.

Dr. Mills said that the 30,000 discrepancies were the only ones he felt to be noteworthy, explaining that there were several hundred thousand discrepancies or contradictions, maybe even a half of million. Conservative commentary that I so easily accepted in bible college seemed to be very weak in giving answers to why we had no writings written by contemporaries of any of the biblical characters. Most of what we were leaning on as proof or evidence came centuries later.

Further troubling, the discovery that the accounts we had used to defend the historicity of Jesus Christ that came from Josephus the historian were fraudulently added by church revisionist poets and historians. Me and my ministry staff's spirits were torn.

One of my ministers brought up how he had found out that the original Trinity appeared to be recorded thousands of years prior to the biblically recorded story we all know today. He stated more startling that the Trinity came out of Africa. Expounding further, he also learned that the God of Ancient Egypt was named Amen or Amun. This was stunning knowing that as a Christian I and every other Christian ended our prayers with the word "Amen." I left our discussion enlightened and perplexed, yet showed the same confidence I showed with my daughter as I was determined to get answers.

Trying to get scholarly answers to these historical questions was not without toil. I and few of my ministers went to every high level theological department of every major educational institution in Chicago.

We started with Moody, Trinity, Wheaton, North Park's theology departments to Loyola, and the University of Chicago. We felt that for sure we would find solid answers in our highest Western Institutions defending Christianity. As a devout minister, understanding the range of liberal vs. conservative, historical vs. mythical theology, I just wanted straightforward answers to my ministry's newly arising questions.

Scholar to Theological professor, from one college to the next university, we as a ministry staff searched for answers to the most essential doctrines to our faith. We had some teacher authorities talk to us about the craftiness of Satan being able to possibly know thousands of years prior about the virgin birth because of prophecy. We were also strongly cautioned by others to not get entangled with some of these "cunning" historical "assertions." I remember wondering at that moment if I was teaching a big fat "cunning assertion."

After regurgitating the same parchment arguments and Carbon 14 Dating methods for scripture verification, they still begged more questions than answers. Also, the other expected "defense arguments" we were given with no direct answers to the questions we posed, was passed troubling for us. A few theologians even knew of the original Trinity. When it came down to it, what all of these theological experts had for me and my staff was that Christianity really just boils down to faith. We learned that Christianity is faith solely because it cannot be proven.

This didn't sit well with me or my ministers. It started to become apparent that our meetings with the top Christian authorities proved more that Christianity came directly from more ancient sources. Thinking about how I was going to tell my wife, family, friends and members that our entire faith is a lie was one of the most frightening of revelations I ever had to give. If not a straight lie, our faith as we knew it was at best a definite unprovable truth. I was devastated with everything that I had learned in light of all the life energy I had dedicated to something that wasn't even certain.

We were diligent to hold on to Jesus and Christianity but were finding ourselves to have less and less evidence and arsenal to truly be able to defend our faith without being illogical, reasonless, and absent of rationale. It was becoming impossible to deduce from the evidence the firm assertions of having an inerrant and authoritative Word of God now.

More disconcerting, was the proclamations and dogma of fundamental doctrine that could be historically proven to have a more original source. Sources of Gnostic (Pagan according to fundamental Christian theology) origin, made it hard to even think about teaching or preaching. These discoveries had me lost.

It was late in the evening; my wife and I were sitting up in bed having pillow talk about my thoughts with all that I was discovering. She was aware of all the new books I had bought, like the books on the apocryphal writings that weren't canonized, to books on ancient African's influence on today's western religions. She had occasionally, hung out and dived in listened while I was watching some DVD's or VHS's on Chiekh Anta Diop, Dr. John Henrik Clarke, or Ashra Kweisi. I began telling her that I could not see myself any longer in good conscience endorsing or teaching Christianity.

After hearing this, she was shattered a second time after just a few months prior hearing my daughter telling her that she believed that Jesus' Virgin Birth was a myth. She was totally aware that we were finding out a lot of questionable things doctrinally as a church and ministry staff, but me like me, she believed that God would provide the answers.

Talking to her with careful and painful contemplation while looking up at the ceiling, I felt alone and spiritually suicidal. I felt like my life had literally jumped off an eternal cliff or a plane flying without radar through amazingly thick endless clouds.

I had to describe to her that as a ministry, we were unable to find any satisfying answers to the questions of original sources of manuscripts, doctrines, or historical characters. That going directly to scholastic African history debunks any possibility of Christianity originating the story of Christ or any of its doctrines. I was unable to hide how learning these things as a Christian and a pastor devastated my entire existence. I was psychologically, spiritually, spatially, and cosmically disoriented and off balance.

I explained that the more I looked at the evidence of faith against reason and giving an unbiased observation of facts, the more I feel like a charlatan teaching the Bible as "God's Word." My wife was outdone! We had gotten together as late teenagers with strong Christian beliefs and had based our entire marriage on Christ and Christian principles.

In my wife's mind, it wasn't really possible to even have real hope for a relationship if the entire relationship came together to empower the very idea that I was now abandoning. At this moment, we had become the most different than we had ever been before.

As far as beliefs and her primary concern was that even when backslidden, I still had Jesus Christ. For me, I no longer had Jesus and inwardly from this point I secretly felt that I no longer had my wife either.

Calling the inevitable meeting with my ministry felt both painful and life altering. As the pastor, along with other ministers who were in their same self-cross examination phase, all of our wives were not inwardly on board understandably.

I was told that I was going to go to hell. I was blamed for intentionally deceiving people. I never thought that I would live to see the day that some who I had led would even dare to call me an infidel, apostate, reprobate, and heretic. My wife held it together and my ministers and their families were never disrespectful or disdainful, at least in my face.

I told everyone that I was not able to continue teaching as a Christian minster for reasons of discovered factual history in direct contradiction to my personal beliefs. Not expounding deeply, but giving brief reason and refraining to disrupt anyone else's beliefs, I shared how I had discovered the most profound knowledge that predates all that we know with so much more to be explored, and left it right there for everyone. I, along with my wife, trustees and officers, formerly dissolved our faith tax exemption status, and at that moment Ark Ministries was no longer a ministry.

So many people were saying so many different things, thinking that the devil had my mind and that I had become a demon possessed heretic. If there was a cross for me in their foremost thoughts, I was the crucified. This was hurtful beyond their comprehension.

Primarily, this was the true beginning of the end of my marriage. At this time, I was more conscience culturally and historically. I now, based on a more conscience diet had become vegan. My hunger for learning everything that I could about my new found discoveries were a direct frustration to my wife. We were on totally different planets, and for the first time I felt that my wife actually believed that I would go to a place called "hell" for not believing in what she believed since a pre-adolescent.

I didn't blame her, but I was intolerant of Christian condemnation, and outright irritated with the audacity of judgment from her, feeling how thorough she knew me theologically. At this boiling point, we tried going to counseling, and because this particular counselor had no fee, she insisted on this Christian psychologist. He started our first session off with a prayer, and needless to say, the entire session didn't go well after that and we had no subsequent sessions with him.

I loved my wife above all. Immaturely, I later became unfaithful to her after not being unfaithful once when I came back to her when we first separated. I was regrettably disrespectful with all she endured, especially me denouncing a faith she was endeared to.

We were both angry with each other for not being where we wanted either one of us to be. Now having two totally opposed life philosophies and spiritual references, we were coming upon our end. Though we loved each other, we were both battling with how we would actually come to what we both knew was the culmination of our entirely Christian based marriage.

Through the emptiness of struggling to maintain relational interest with one another, moving away from everyone, we moved all the way out to the northwest suburbs of Chicago, where we met our finale. Not doing right by her, she rightfully wanting revenge and freedom to unfaithfulness, we separated and later divorced.

Now I was a single father, a former pastor, and an official

loner for the first time. I was now free to anything and everything that I wished, free to the streets, free to women, or free to any whim that I might have. However, this freedom experienced within this context was overwhelming and over rated.

I struggled to get my bearings, and moved in with my friend Jah Ranu Menab in Hyde Park. I stayed between there, my friend Heru in Calumet City, my people on 64th and S. Evans or family on 64th and Cottage Grove. Feeling all over the place, this was a very difficult time for me, yet a very self-reflecting time.

I thought about all of the things that I could have done to save my marriage, and thought about how life would actually be moving forward. I thought about how I could still be a great father to my three beautiful children. For the first time in my entire life, I really recognized now that the fog was gone forever.

# CHAPTER THIRTEEN

## *The Fog is Gone*

Here I am, with no God to name, no faith and no family, for the first time since being a late teenager, and truly now on my own. Based on a decision to move on from my wife caused the initial agony from being permanently in a different home than my children. Envisioning the future as positively as I could mentally muster, I thought that they will at least be able to visit me and maybe stay with me some time out of the year throughout the years.

It seemed poetic to now be moving in with my close friend from Moody Bible Institute. He was an exceptional

120

student at MBI and yet had long abandoned the doctrines he learned there, changed his name, and was now adept in the knowledge of ancient Egyptian history and rituals.

His new blessed name was Jah Ranu Menab. Jah like I, had collected thousands of books throughout the years, yet he had an astounding amount of books on Black culture both ancient and current. Besides moving into Hyde Park which is the Black Conscious Community's hub in Chicago, having Frontline Book store around the corner from me, I had my brother who similarly recently divorced his wife and had moved passed Christianity to a high level of enlightenment.

The condo that we lived in was a larger three bedrooms, hard wood floors, high ceilings and was one of eight units in the four stories, dark brick pre-modern style building. To be expected we had furnishings befitting to two recently made bachelors. My room was embarrassingly skeletal. Bare necessities like clothes and simple bedding, reminded me of dormitory days that I had long left behind. However, deep within, regardless of unfamiliarity and discomfort, I knew that all would eventually be well in my life.

I began taking the time, without TV, and relational distractions to read without interruption. I became familiar with Jah's library and was awakened to new concepts and history that had managed to evade me and my whole life of study up until this point. I spent major hours and money at Frontline book store on 53rdand Harper, analyzing, evaluating, and internalizing the deep discoveries of my people's hidden history. I was exposed to the ancient priesthood of Waset, the history of Ta Seti, Kenset, Kemet, all the way up to the time of the Moors. It was like awakening a new life with so much more to uncover.

Not knowing what to do with all that I was learning, I was still experiencing a deep state of cognitive dissonance, So many life altering circumstances taking place in my life in such a short period of time, I was looking for something stable. Deep down within I knew that I needed to really get to know me and for the most part I was guarded about that.

Well sort of. I had gotten involved with a woman and we started doing a sales business together. I went back and forth with her about getting a place together as she was trying to rush me to create a new relationship and family with her. I was not really ready as she already had two children close to the age of my youngest son. Not admitting at first, it was hard trying to spend time with her and her children feeling the pain of not being with mine everyday anymore.

Regarding this very brief jaunt with this lady, I learned a lot about what I truly wanted in a relationship. There's a lot of my family and friends who stayed in a very rough area off of Cottage Grove where I spent a lot of days and nights. She didn't like me being in that area and would try to control me from going there.

So there was the issue of her controlling ways and my close proximity of not having my bearings individually. I finally became fed up and I couldn't believe that I was even entertaining someone so close, time wise, out of my marriage. I understood thoroughly what I was doing was simply filling a void. In this brief and horrible attempt at an apparent rebounding relationship, I was now fully aware of what I would or wouldn't be willing to tolerate moving forward.

Digging deeper into my new found livelihood I eventually met a woman who wanted to be the queen mother wife and provide me with multiple wives. Although flattered I quickly declined this opportunity, as this was not something I was willing to entertain and had no real need for a relationship of this magnitude.

Feeling even more lost without being in any relationship, I tried a few excursions with a few females only finding myself wanting to be by myself more and more. This time of a crushing sense of lost-ness, I had underestimated the difficulties of actually being alone.

I went back to hanging out on the block with all that that entails. Jah saw me a few times needing to grab my guns out of the house to tend to negatively created drama. At the moment of transition, to do or be whatever I ever wanted to be or do, or even what a lot of Christians expected me to do, I saw myself very clouded with this new space of being alone & free.

Jah would just strongly implore me to be careful, but knew that he couldn't caution me like he once could when we abided by the rule of Christian doctrine. My brother had just become an initiate into an ancient priestly order, and for me, I was not ready for that type of commitment because all the knowledge that I was learning was so new. It became a psychological struggle with all of the lies I had been taught via my programmed upbringing in my Western oriented education and indoctrination. I was both now awakened but recklessly clueless to consciousness and to which direction I should take in life.

Living with my brother Jah, I discovered that I was too close to too many women on lower nature attractions and too close to the temptations from my family and friends on the block. I saw myself being inundated into a surreal state of nothingness.

Seeing myself, I knew that I needed to make a swift change as everybody still dying and getting locked up on the block, as usual. I made a decision moving forward to spend most of my time out of the city in a south suburb called Calumet City to stay with my brother Heru. He lived in a house by himself and invited me to stay with him to get out of Hyde Park and the hood.

This was crucial for me, because there was peace and quiet in his home and he was also conscience and prioritized a life of meditation. He explained that he was preparing himself for his wife or wives and  was not entertaining casual options. He never brought a women or anybody for that fact to his home, ever.

Heru viewed his home as sacred, and he believed that I was supposed to be there at his home in light of all that I was going through in my life. I noticed immediately that I was still guided divinely to be right where I needed to be in this time. Our schedules never allowed us to see each other much, maybe once every few days.

It was here, that I spent many day and night meditating on life and all that I had learned. Here I learned the sacred gift of silence, and the stillness of the mind. I began to grasp that if I wanted order without, then that would require that I had to attain order within. I felt that all that I was going through internally was pushing to build on these lessons learned.

Literally, I began looking at the entire world differently. I would take long walks every night on the Indiana side of Stateline Street in a very serene neighborhood. When I went into the city, I would take endless walks up and down the lake of South Shore beaches and would just listen to the water crashing up against the rocks.

On these long walks, I thought about how I could reshape

my life with my thoughts. I thought about how I was now a teacher without anyone to teach. I thought about how much I loved Hiphop but gave it all up for Jesus & my family. I thought about how great of a man I knew that I could be for a woman. In light of my ability to be a beast in the streets, I thought about how many people's lives in this same environment had been transformed and how these same people loved and respected me.

All along, I had developed this deep ethereal notion that I was born with a great purpose to impact the culture of Black people. Throughout all my different life experiences and being deeply inducted into the fog, I never lost my inner compass to awaken and teach my people. I knew that we as a people have been through so much. From Hiphop to ministry, to now being awakened to truth, I was looking for every specific detail to uncover the elixirs needed to heal the current conditions and the cellular and genetic memory of my people.

One day back at Heru's house, while relaxing on the couch, I noticed that my mail had piled up for weeks. Thumbing through multiple envelopes, I came to a markedly distinguished piece of mail. Attentively scanning this letter, I shockingly noticed that it was returned addressed to me from a long lost music executive that I knew back in California. I opened it up, and the letter in essence said that he already had my songs from one of my previous albums. He further expressed that he would like to submit them for his current major distribution deal that he was working on with Universal Records.

Within this letter, there was a brief overview of contractual percentages and allocations. On the bottom of the letter he put his phone contact which I hadn't had for years. I eagerly called him and after hearing his familiar voice pick up, with great excitement we caught up with each other and then we discussed more details about the distribution deal.

He advised that if I wanted to come to California to record some new material, he would be glad to see me, and believed this could add more leverage for me in this deal. This all seemed to drop out of the sky on me. Going about my life as I knew it, I was now instantly exploring totally new options that I wasn't even considering before.

It was close to ten years since I had been back in California. It was a mental therapy just contemplating the thought of being in California with its beautiful year round climate from the unpredictable and unpleasant weather of Chicago. Never totally away from Hip-hop, only by recording, in deep imagination and thought, I was pondering what type of explosive and powerful lyrics I would drop if I got back in the studio.

For weeks I pondered on the decision. I remember not having a car, feeling the overwhelming need for a change of Calumet City's scenery. I took the Pace bus to the CTA

(Chicago's Transit Authority bus and subway lines) and went to hang out with all my people back on the block.

One day on Cottage Grove. I talked to one of my forever friends, which he's more like a brother to me. We all endearingly refer to him as Mo Fresh Kobe Jordan Air Wade because of his basketball and lyrical skills.

For several days of him seeing me in the hood, coming and sleeping on the floor of his apartment, knowing my history and knowing about the letter I had recently received, he was determined to tell me repeatedly to get back to California. He came to me with a list of the reasons why I should leave Chicago. Then he would list all of the benefits I would have being in California.

Finally, I told him that I would more than likely go to California for a couple of weeks. Just glad for any commitment from me to go, his attitude and response was plainly, "good, now go!" He was vocal in saying how he hated seeing me waste my time in Chicago when he felt that I was greater than every emcee in Hiphop, and could easily take over the entire rap industry. Every minute of every hour, "get out of here Aki'" he would tell me. We called each other Ak' referencing the Arabic word Akhi or Hebrew word Achi meaning my brother.

I spent some time with my children, tied up all my loose ends in Chicago, packed up a suit case and prepared myself for my flight to California. I told Heru that I was leaving and what opportunity I was exploring, and that I would more than likely be back in a few weeks. Heru said that this opportunity could possibly lead to so many other bigger things. Just as uncertain as I was, we both held high conscience optimism toward my future prospects.

Strangely, I think that we both kind of knew that I was catapulting my life into a new dimension. I definitely knew that I was moving into the unknown. In some extraordinary space, I felt as though I was literally metamorphosing a new beginning of existence and was peculiarly looking ahead to the western horizon and now seeing far beyond the fog.

# CHAPTER FOURTEEN
## *Beyond the Fog*

"What is this fog" you may still be wondering since it hasn't been defined once yet in this book? Some right off knows exactly the parallels I am drawing between Christianity and the fog. My formal definition comes by the way of an acronym of the word "fog." F.O.G. as being alluded to throughout this book from the first chapter is referred to as the "Fabrications of God." This fog I can further elucidate with this acronym as the "Fictions of God" or even the "Falsifications of God."

This was the mysterious fog that was running the backdrop of my life. This was the fog that hides the truth and presents its own reality. This fog is but the thick illusory religious clouds that hides the clear view of the glorious sun or the magnificent starry night sky.

Christianity was introduced to me in a form when I was very young. I realized that I was not born with Christianity directly, and that my first experience with church looking back didn't resonate with the young natural part of me. It was intriguing and life altering for me as a late teenager in need of something positive, from only seeing my entire life through the lens of my upbringing. Looking beyond the F.O.G. now, I realized that I was as every bit godly from conception and I was breathing God's very breath at birth.

Oddly, the small toddler memories I retained were the shadowy snapshots of my amazement of the morning sun and the strange fear of the darkness of night. Experiencing both cold and hot climates and not knowing them as neither normal nor unusual. Just totally at peace and flowing with all situations. Being in this inexperienced stage where I was honest with pain and discomfort, and in the next instant, letting go the pain and immediately being unrestrained to smile or have outburst of laughter.

The memories that stay fresh with me are the times of always laying right up under my mother in her bed. I can still mentally evoke her scent, her voice, her choice of music while she would at most nights, be holding a book reading under the dim lamp on her night stand.

I have both sharp and abstract nostalgias of my pre-toddler stage of exploring all of the rooms in my house without having names or labels for anything. Just being able to go back in the mental memory and recall looking at something ignorantly, to looking at that very same thing with thorough knowledge is divine. Just having this ability for cerebral recall and perception depth is amazing. Someone has said, "It's not what you are looking at, it's what you see."

It was later that I learned while growing into the age of a post toddler that my mom's name was Carlyn and my dad's name was Nate Baby. My sister who grew up in the house with me was name Debbie. We all lived in a house in a city called Cleveland, Ohio. The name my parents named me was Nathaniel McCrary named after my dad, and my mom endearingly called me Nicky (no one in the family could ever draw the parallel of my government name to my nickname).

At this post toddler stage, I can recall how I learned that I had to formally acquire the English language, have house chores, given social expectations, and school requirements. I was being introduced to the programming of my parents influenced directly from their own programming. These post toddler years psychologist refer to as the most formable years that help determine the rest of one's life.

Growing up in my generation we started off with

television programs then began our assimilation into the school programs, with the lunch programs, and the after school programs. This educational program was psychologically perilous for a young Black child in the urban school system hoping to gain self-confidence toward life and the future. I remember my brainwashed introduction to the Pledge of Allegiance, to the flag, under God, with a preparatory government and religious program that I didn't feel included me or my people.

However, my earliest memories as a child are those that recall an awareness of self without markers or classifications. I'm referring to the memories that are hazy thoughts of pre-language indoctrinations and worldly or societal influences. I see on different levels that I was being shaped by the environment that I was born into. I can also see from the level of my new born innocence and inexperience coming into my new world, the gradual contamination of a pure soul and mind.

I had no true attachment to my name, citizenship status, city or state of birth, regional location, food preference, and lifestyle requirements. I was only devoted to breathing and a need for love, and I was truly just me. I was unprejudiced by liking one person more than the other as I was learning at the highest form how to read peoples energies as they were. My earliest memories of childhood show the most pure state of divine clarity evading all forms of inclement fog.

As children, none of us had doctrines about breathing. We had no books to reference about love. There were no rituals on feeling hungry to be learned. Laughter and sadness were exhibited without being attributed to a god or a devil. Every one of us, without the voices from the outside world, is primarily and practically a pure conscience being.

Now that I am no longer a pastor or a Christian for that fact, the first thing people like to ask me mostly is, "what do you believe in now?" Or "Do you believe in God at all?" My response is rather wide-ranging depending on the context of the question. In short form to those who are curious, let me broad sweepingly answer both question and questions of the like. I believe in myself, my ancestors, in nature, and I believe in God.

More typical and specifically following the prior questions, I'm frequently asked, "Do you still believe in Jesus and the Bible? Here, I'm not so eclectic as I'm very forthright that the Jesus Christ referred to in scripture is a hybrid of the most ancient Heru the KRST from Kemet. He was the first KRST who became so many variants in other ancient cultures postdating this original account.

Even more straightforward regarding the Bible, its reliability, inerrancy, and authority being proclaimed as "God's Word," is for any well researched free thinking person, laughable. The Bible also has a multitude of ancient sources with an enormous amount of textual variations and inconsistencies, rendering the understanding of these scriptures useless to true interpretation. This makes most conservative Western Bible scholars suspect as they are being dogmatic on solid uncertainties.

Nonetheless, let me pre-emptively state my public handling of these issues before ending this chapter and book. I am neither a self-professed scholar nor a debater against any of the western religions. I plainly happened to become a former devout Christian, minister, and pastor.

Based on my own research, and consequent conclusions, I chose not to follow any longer the teachings or doctrines of this religion, nor believe any of its condemnations. I thoroughly knew and practiced my faith and later discovered the true origins of my beliefs. After which, grounded on my experience and continued spiritual and cultural teaching in other directions, I decided to write a book about it, and here it is.

For me, this freedom from religion to what I consider to be a greater level of spiritual enlightenment, awakening, and conscious free thinking is not up for debate. Because of the fact that I currently teach Black people in particular about their ancient culture, I have been considered demon possessed, a heretic, a reprobate, an infidel, and an apostate. All of these deeply engrained damning labeling techniques against anyone opposing or challenging "the faith" are pathetically ineffective. I literally equal it to a child sincerely telling me on the night of December 24th, that I need to go to sleep or Santa will not come.

Maybe you have read my book up until this point and you are now convinced that I deserve such name calling and epithets. That would not be unexpected with the commitment in our society to these beliefs systems. On the other hand, maybe you have read this book and find yourself at the crossroads. As I have written about earlier, I am fully familiar with this life's intersection that is blindingly dangerous in this dense fog with unseen traffic.

Maybe the dogmatic views that you once held are starting to unravel. Like in my experience, you feel more alone than you could have ever imagined. At least in the fog, it was all figured out for you with a book, a belief, and a God you had been given a name for. Perhaps just considering beyond these seemingly fixed truths is too much to even think about. Truth is subjective. Facts can be made up or dug up. I dug up facts.

You see, when I became enlightened on classical history verses biblical or traditional history, it painfully exposed my religious beliefs. I couldn't even imagine what any type of alternatives looked like for the overall spiritual meaning of my life. After going through excruciating psychological and confusing spiritual pain, for the first time like when we were babies, I was back to learning who I was without any categories. My name, my religion, my education, my socialization, and my entire definition of me, had become my several different existences of me in various bubbles of sorts.

These social categorizations gave splices of insight to certain aspects of me. Yet, these shallow titles of existence did nothing to help describe the deeper parts of me that ironically only I could ever know. The majority of my whole life, I later realized that I had been defining myself with these external markers while ignoring the true inner me.

This truth gave me a raw sense that there was this deep and silent part of me that doesn't have a name, a language, or an emotion. So, the most powerful question that was self-imposed by me to me was "Who am I?"

Without ancient or current geographical claim, without racial cataloguing, without family name, educational, or financial status, I asked myself "Who am I?"

This question is one of four Master Keys that I will give in concluding this book. This question "Who am I," is the number one Master Key to releasing you from the realm of the F.O.G. that permeates your life. In all of your programming, you have never been prodded, educated, encouraged, trained, or raised to ask "Who am I?" You like I, have been told who and what we were from all aspects of a socially engineered society.

I truly believe that this question "Who am I" is the deepest question one can ask her or himself. I also believe that it doesn't take a lifetime to answer it, but several. This is when you learn that secret serene unmovable, eternal, immutable, and unnameable part of you. When you ask "Who am I" you learn that the higher non-judgmental part of you is the very one observing the compartmentalized and categorized you trying to figure out what this thing called life is all about.

You know that you are an individual. But you don't know what the word individual really means. This lack of knowledge prevented you from truly knowing you. Not going too esoterically deep on etymological meanings in common root words but this is the *indivisible duality* that makes you an Indivi<u>dual</u> (dual meaning two parts). Stop for a few seconds before reading on and formally introduce yourself to your higher self with the words of life, prosperity, and health. Now, appreciate the experience of this new alert duality within yourself that's totally undivided.

Now on to the second Master Key. The second Master Key to being free from the fog is an understanding that you are and have always been a divine being from birth. You were not born into sin or unrighteousness. Your environment might have had social constructs that disadvantage one group over another, but this is not reflective of your divine inward nature. A plain spiritual deduction is that all life is created by a Divine source and thereby making all life Divine.

This might be a major paradigm shift for you but one of the most crucial ones to grasp. Please note that there is some good in the most evil of people and some evil in the most good of people. These good or evil patterns are based on learned or unlearned behavior and personal choices, not inborn traits.

We have been indoctrinated that we find our way to God by praying that "It" will come to us and fill us with "it's" spirit. The truth is that God is within and has always been there. The truth is that until we have a quiet mind, it is impossible to hear "Her" and I'll leave that right there.

The third Master Key is research. Maybe I have exposed a new street to explore for your personal journey. Maybe you feel that I have made a lot of disclaimers to things you hold dear and true. Or maybe this book resonates with you but you just don't know which way to go. Understand that you won't learn everything overnight and that you are in a society that has never even prompted you to know your inner Self but just the opposite.

Research leads to enlightenment and is crucial to penetrate deeper levels of consciousness. There is no Bible to become awakened. With that being said, there is so much richness of investigation with accurate evidence on ancient spiritual cultures that prove to be the original essence of what we get in piece and form in these more recent western religions.

I think that this point is crucial to Black people. It has been said that if you want to hide something from a Black person, all you have to do is put it in a book. Before we vehemently disagree with this assumption against us, we have to acknowledge our cultural behavior patterns. Before we become upset with how we have been so grossly deceived, we must consider why? Are Blacks not in this state of continued controlled confusion collectively because we don't research?

As far as cultural healing for Blacks around the world, all we need to do is go back and review our most uncorrupted part of our collective history. The late (German bought scholar) Egyptologist Dr. E.A. Wallace Budge said that the more he went back in ancient Egypt, the more Black and the more pure the culture became. Actually, seeing our ancient culture as Blacks will breathe life into us to become our best current culture possible. And the truth is that we don't have to go any further back than ancient Nubia to trace all that we need to know for growing back into a spiritual high culture again. Research, research, and research!

The last crucial Master Key I will give is meditation. Before I spook you off, know that there are so many different aspects of meditation. I digress here to say though, if there is ever going to be any collective healing for Blacks in America, we have to heal our ancestors. For those of us who are alive, we have the responsibility to heal our ancestors. If we don't, we are destined to stay sick spiritually and culturally.

Meditation can range all the way from ancestral connection and astral travel to simple calming practices. In practical application, meditating is vital to silencing the busy mind and does wonders for your health. Whatever you might be going through personally, if it's not causing an imminent direct danger to you physically, it is therefore only an attribute of the mind. Meditation helps heal this type of psychosis hindering your very love of life.

Eckhart Tolle wrote powerfully in the book *The Power of Now*, that to be overly concerned with what happened years ago, last year, last month, last week, yesterday, or the last hour or minute to second, is the major cause of insanity. Equally, over concern or worry about anytime in the near or distant future is mentally reckless. His premise echoing the teachings of ancient times is to always be in the present.

There is also a lot of truth to the statement that you are what you think you are. But this statement is but a half or partial truth. At a deeper level, your thoughts are but a small fraction of your entire mind or entire being. It is true that if you are all over the place mentally you will also be all over the place in life. The master key is to learn to quiet the mind so that your thoughts can first be silenced and controlled by your higher mind. Up until knowing this, you might have been inclined to pride yourself in having such a busy mind.

Uncontrolled thoughts and a busy mind is the main culprit that is hiding us from our deeper selves and inner peace and power. I think it is important to start off with a simple calming private session for at least fifteen to twenty minutes a day. Try to find a consistent peaceful place if possible where you can get away and sit upright or lay back in silence.

At first your thoughts will race across your frontal mental space like a congested interstate in rush hour traffic. This is the challenge on a journey to a quiet mind. You have to let your thoughts pass like clouds and hold no judgment on any particular thought, one way or the other. Just let your thoughts pass by.

Overtime, this will give you more governance over your thought patterns which will also help you go wherever you want to go mentally and in life. Meditation will eventually lead you to deeper inner truths that will give you confident control over your newly discovered abilities. All this regarding meditation and a busy mind makes true this summary of the Buddha saying, "Our lives are shaped by our minds, we become what we think."

Through being more self-aware, spiritually conscience, and culturally awake, your soul can forever leave the realm of the F.O.G. There is much noise and confusion about what it truly means to be awake. To be awakened is not a collection of facts, nor is housed in much knowledge. At its core it means an awareness to see our oneness with everyone and everything around us. Being awake is having a crystal clear view of life in all of its many manifestations. There is no F.O.G. in knowing that the God in me honors the God in you.

Webster's dictionary defines fog as: "A thick cloud of water droplets suspended in the atmosphere at or near the earth's surface that obscures or restricts visibility (to a greater extent than mist; strictly reducing visibility to below one kilometer)." The Fabrications of God that I speak about in this book restricts visibility to things we have never seen clearly before. When the F.O.G. is lifted or disintegrated, we can see things that were once hidden. When the F.O.G. is gone we can move with confidence and less caution on the scenic route of life.

You might struggle with different information in different ways dealing with the same doctrines or beliefs from Western religions. Because of cognitive dissonance or a concern with what others think can delay one's awakening or keep one sleep. Some people take a life time to wake up, and some never do. Everyone has their own process.

When I left ministry and eventually moved away to California from Chicago, I found my destiny and healing. I now have my Eternal Beautiful Goddess Mysaidees who

I praise and adore. Together, we are raising our goddess and god which are our two youngest. I now have five amazing gods total, two female and three male. My divine linage is all very close with one another and they all love each other immensely.

My Goddess, Mysaidees is a strong force behind Self Centered Society; a society I formed that teaches individuals to be centered within the Self. She also fuses me with life and inspiration to speak, teach, and write and bring elevation to our culture. She is so much more than a woman, she is God! Only if you are currently awake can this truth vibrate with you.

For those of you who are already awake. I want to say thank you for all your support and love. If nothing else, this book helps you know a little bit more about me personally and can be a great resource to family or friends who you know are still in or struggling with the F.O.G. Sometimes people might need to see someone be vulnerable enough to expose what they have struggled with to help them become free. There are a lot of people, who are just plain afraid of being labeled demonic or crazy, believe me I know.

So, if you are fresh on your journey out of the F.O.G., or you are just inspired by what you've read, please visit me on my website: www.temelkarango.com. On my page, you will find my itinerary and all of my contact information. Also, there are resources and links to assist you if you are on your new found quest. For those of you who are more adept consciously and are maybe looking for a platform to build with the focus on bringing the highest level of culture through enlightenment, you found it.

With that being said, I'll end with these words to everyone: to become truly Self-centered means to intimately know your Higher Self. Those who are Masters of themselves truly know that when you know Yourself, it is the only true Door to knowing God. Learning your Higher Holy Inner Self, or as the mystics say, your Holy Guardian, is to learn the hidden Holy Spirit that cannot be found in the doctrines of men.

The theologian nor the philosopher, the religious nor the physicist, the psychologist nor the spiritualist presents the true door to the Substantial Reality underlining us all and the Omni verses. We must go within. There is no higher spiritual height that can be attained without knowledge of Self. This is the greatest gift that we can ever receive in life, Ourselves. Hopefully, in all that you have read, I have begun the journey of given You the gift of You back to You!

So to all who look with your two eyes at this book's concluding words, know that you can only See with the one Eye that gives pure understanding, that you are DIVINE! May you awaken to know it, àse!

*-Temel Karango*

# *Acknowledgements*

First and foremost, I'd like to express a grand acknowledgement to my Goddess Marsaidees Burney. She's my project manager, personal assistant, and my absolute everything! Without you, this book would not have come to fruition. Thank you my love for your love, support, and your life! I want to recognize my beautiful children, Atossa, Tre, Josiah, Jada, and Amir for understanding my sacrifice to be a Light-Worker, and having to share your father with the rest of the world. I love all of you more than life itself!

Thanks to my big sister Deborah for loving me wherever I was in life. Thanks to my sister Laqwana for the same. Thank you to Sernard for being my brother and for being there with me through my many life journeys. To my big bro Willie Lee, love and gratitude as you have always been more solid than a rock to me. A huge word of recognition to my brother Jah Ranu Menab, who wrote the forward to this book, and who has had a great influence on me and who will forever be family.

Thanks and love to Mo Fresh, as you have always pushed me to live my greatest Self. Lil bro Bam (James Gabb), I want to salute you for always reminding me to be patient in route to greatness. Recognition is definitely due to my big brother Clifford Alston in Atlanta, for you always being a conscience mind and feeding me knowledge and arsenal for uplifting our people.

I want to give a special thank you to those who were with me at the inception of Self Centered Society: My brother *The Messenger,* Jesse Caver (Chicago Headquarters Coordinator), and Adam Foster (the big, big brother). Thank you sister Kimistry Awake! You have decades of commitment to our people, and I thank you for your support and for you being a teacher's teacher.

Thank you Sister Dorothy Morgan, I look forward to your teachings. Thanks for the support from my lil' brother, Tony Rush, we have a lot of work to do together. Brother Heru, I am grateful for you for being a High Priest to me in preparing me for my ancestral work. I must acknowledge my brother Jarrod for always being a great light in my life.

I also want recognize my sister Meiko Drew for your expert direction in marketing. Darlene Tate thanks for giving guidance to my organizational needs towards my personal business growth. I would like to give a big acknowledgement to Brother Dennis Burnside, who helped in the initial editing of this book, and who would travel across state lines to support me in uplifting our people

Lastly, I want to show honor to all of you have supported my transformation and teaching all around the country and the world via social media. Strength, love, and support to the pastors, ministers, and Christians who reach out to me with their questions toward enlightenment. Those who have grown and continue to help strengthen us at Self-Centered Society, infinite love and gratitude!

www.ingramcontent.com/pod-product-compliance
Lightning Source LLC
Chambersburg PA
CBHW071344090426
42738CB00012B/3002